Acting Duologues

for boys & girls aged 5-10yrs

Compiled and edited by Kim Gilbert

Dramatic Arts Studio Publications

Copyright © 2021
Kim Gilbert All rights
reserved
ISBN: 9798486973024

DEDICATION

This collection of acting duologues is dedicated to all teachers and students of drama with a love of performing. There is something for every young performer to choose from. The characters in this book have been chosen carefully and are most suited to boys and girls within the 5-10 yr age range. The dialogue is mainly simple and the characters and plots are taken mostly from a range of fairy tales which children of this age love to read and perform. These scenes are suitable for a wide range of study, performance, exams and festivals.

ACKNOWLEDGEMENTS

A special thank you goes to my husband Steve, who has prepared this collection of scenes for publication.

TABLE OF CONTENTS

Introduction	7
Acting a role	9
Acting Style, Fantasy, Comedy	10
Duo Acting	11
The Three Little Pigs	13

<u>The Wizard of Oz:</u>

The Good Witch & Dorothy	16
Dorothy & Scarecrow	20
Dorothy & Scarecrow (2)	23
Dorothy & Tin Man	26
Dorothy & Lion	29
Pinocchio & Geppetto	32

<u>Pinocchio:</u>

Pinocchio & Jiminy Cricket	35
Pinocchio & the Fairy	38
Tom Sawyer & Ben	41
The Miller & Puss	43

<u>Toad of Toad Hall:</u>

Marigold & her Nurse	49
Rat & Mole	53

Mole & Rat	57
Ratty & Mole	63
Phoebe & Toad	67
Toad & Ratty	71
Winnie the Pooh:	
Rabbit & Winnie the Pooh	75
Kanga & Roo	79
Peter Pan	84
Beauty and the Beast	90
The Little Mermaid & the Witch	96
Red Riding Hood & the Wolf	98
Alice in Wonderland:	
Alice & the Cheshire Cat	101
Alice & the Caterpillar	104
Alice & the Pigeon	108
The Leopard & the Ethiopian	111
Nelis & Kobus	115
Wicked Queen & Snow White	118
Tyltyl & the Child	120
The Town Mouse & the Country Mouse	126
The Hare & the Tortoise	129
Mr & Mrs Beaver	132
The Princess & the Woodcutter	136

INTRODUCTION

I have compiled and edited this collection of Classic duologues for young boys and girls to read, perform and enjoy. These scenes are suitable for a range of acting exams and awards as well as for auditions and festivals. I have tried and tested these scenes with numerous young students over the years with great success and more importantly, my students have thoroughly enjoyed working on them. It is so important to choose characters within ones' playing range. This collection of duologues contain a range of characters suited to be played by young boys and girls from the age of approximately 5yrs to 10 yrs. From my experience, I have seen many young actors tackling characters which are often unsuited to their age range and skills. These scenes are within the range of younger children who have just started on their journey of learning to read fluently and enjoy performing.

There will be plenty of time in the future to tackle the more mature and demanding male characters which are available to play from a wealth of drama and literature. Students need to learn to build their skills and technique slowly and systematically and start their journey with the younger, and more age- appropriate characters before attempting to move forwards to the demands of older and more complex characters.

The duologues in this collection are taken from a range of plays and classic novels: The Three Little Pigs, Red Riding Hood, Snow White, Peter Pan, The Wizard of Oz, The Wind in the Willows, Winnie the Pooh, Pinocchio, Beauty & the Beast, Aesops fables and many more. Each scene has an introduction prepared suitable for exam or festival work and are also timed with exams and festival work in mind. The duologues within this book are suitably short and manageable for a younger age group. I hope you enjoy this collection!

ACTING A ROLE

Here are some questions to consider when acting a role:

Is your character a main character in the story?

Consider what your character looks like in terms of physical appearance? This can be considered in terms of age, height, and posture. Perhaps you could draw a picture of your character, imagining what she or he looks like.

What does your character look like in costume? Is your character a fantasy character? Imagine the costume your character might wear and draw a picture.

How does your character sound? Is your natural voice appropriate or do you need to characterise your voice and speak with an accent? Explore using your voice in different ways to create your character's unique voice.

What happens to your character in the story? If you do not have a lot of information about your character try to create his or her back story. Perhaps you could try writing your own script for the character you are playing.

What does your character like to do or dislike doing?

How do you relate to your character and how does your character relate to the other characters in the play or story?

What are the things you like about your character?

Consider casting. Is this role a good choice for you? Does this character suit your acting skills and personality?

ACTING STYLE

It is important to adopt the correct style of acting for your chosen performance piece. Many plays for young children are based on comedy or fantasy.

FANTASY

This style of acting has no limitations. In fantasy, anything can happen and the actor has great scope to use his or her imagination. This style is not to be taken too seriously and offers the young actor great creativity. Many children's plays involve fantasy and are a popular choice with younger players. Therfore, these types of plays are a good starting point for young actors. The style of acting is often larger than life and 'overacting' in these types of roles is common and acceptable.

COMEDY

Comedy is writing which is written with the intention of making people laugh. It can include jokes and humorous situations which are often far from real life. If realism is employed, it is usually a heightened form of realism. Children love comedy in general. They often love a larger-than-life slap stick humour.

DUO ACTING

Duo acting involves two actors and therefore it is essential to build up a rapport with the person you are going to be acting with. A trust and confidence in each other is essential and it will be necessary to find time to rehearse together as well as preparing apart. It is ideal and equally important to choose a scene which suits both players strengths and which has a balanced amount of text for each speaker. It is preferable for each actor to play only one role. Duo acting is great fun and is a good way of learning to respond, share and communicate with each other. Duologues are extremely rewarding as well as useful to work on with students in drama classes and most examination boards and drama festivals offer a range of duo acting examinations. There is a range of material in this book aimed at stimulating and stretching young actors. I have provided a short but useful introduction to the scenes setting the scenes in context and there are limited stage directions. I believe the actor will work towards understanding the scene within the context of the play as a whole and work creatively towards staging these scenes in their own unique way. Equally, the locations can be adapted to your personal preference as long as they work appropriately.

THE THREE LITTLE PIGS
Adapted by Kim Gilbert

(Mother Pig is giving some worldly advice to her eldest son as he makes his journey out into the world alone).

Mother Pig:
Now, my son, as you are my eldest son, it is high time that you learned to make your way in the world. You need to learn to become independent. One day, you may have a family of your own to take care of. And it is my job to prepare you how to do that.

Eldest son:
But I like it here, mother. I love living with you and my two brothers. I feel safe. And besides, I love your cooking. There will be so much for me to learn. Do you think I will be able to do it?

Mother Pig:
I know you will, son. I will miss you too. But it is important that you learn to stand on your own two feet. Everyone has to learn to do this someday. You can't live with your mother forever.

Eldest son:
Do I really have to go? I'm not ready.

Mother Pig:
You are going to be fine. You are a big, strong pig – and smart too. And so handsome! Look at your neat curly hair and your cute little twiddly tail. You will find that you know more than you think you do for I have taught you well.

Eldest son:
I'm going to miss you, mother. And I'm going to miss your dumplings. Will you teach me to make dumplings before I go?

Mother Pig:
Of course, I will, my son.

Eldest son:
But where will I find a suitable place to live?

Mother Pig:
You will need to find a safe place. Somewhere where there's plenty of space to grow your own food - and don't forget water – you will need water. Water is essential for life. And then, of course, you will have to start to build yourself a home.

Eldest Son:
But how will I do that?

Mother Pig:
I have been saving up money for you and your brothers since you were small and cute little piglets. It's time for me to give it to you now and it will be up to you how you spend it. But please – be sure to spend it wisely.

Eldest Son:
You can be sure I will spend it wisely. I will build myself a house of bricks. Even though bricks are more expensive, bricks will last much longer than wood or straw. In the long run, my house will keep me safe. Please mother, when it is finished, you must come and visit. Perhaps you would like to live with me when you see what a strong and pleasant house I've built.

Mother Pig:
That I most certainly will. Oh - and one more word of advice. You must beware of the big bad wolf who lives in the forest. Many of your poor relatives have been tricked by him and have never lived to tell the tale.

Eldest Son:
I have heard those stories many times, Mother. And that is why I am going to build my house of bricks unlike my cousins who wasted their money on straw and wood. My house will be built so strong that it will keep out any old wolf which comes my way. And when it is built, I will find a way to keep that nasty old wolf away forever.

Mother Pig:
That might be easier said than done, son.

<u>Eldest Son:</u>
You wait and see. I already have a plan. He won't be eating roasted pork, you'll see. I will be serving you and my brothers, delicious Wolf Soup!

THE WIZARD OF OZ
by L. FRANK BAUM

(After a huge cyclone, Dorothy finds herself over the rainbow. The first person she meets is the Good Witch of the North. Unfortunately, there are still the Wicked Witches of the East and the West for Dorothy to contend with).

Good Witch:
You are welcome, most noble Sorceress, to the Land of Munchkins.

Dorothy:
You are very kind.

Good Witch:
We are grateful to you for having killed the Wicked Witch of the East and for setting our people free from her spell.

Dorothy:
But there must be some mistake. I haven't killed anyone.

Good Witch:
Well, your house did, and that is the same thing. See! There are the witch's shoes, still sticking out from underneath it.

Dorothy:
Oh dear, the house was blown away by a strong wind. It must have fallen on her. What shall we do?

Good Witch:
Nothing. There is nothing we can do. She was wicked and paid for her wickedness. Now that she is dead, the Munchkins are all free and happy again.

Dorothy:
But who are the Munchkins?

Good Witch:
They are the people who live in the Land of the East where the wicked witch rules.

Dorothy:
Are you a Munchkin?

Good Witch:
(She laughs). No, but I am their friend. I am the Witch of the North.

Dorothy:
Oh, dear! Are you really a witch?

Good Witch:
Yes, indeed, but I am a good witch and the people love me. I am not as powerful as the Wicked Witch was, or I should have set the people free myself.

Dorothy:
But I thought all witches were wicked.

Good Witch:
Oh no! You are making a great mistake. There are wizards too. Oz himself is a great Wizard. He is more powerful than all the rest of us put together. He lives in the City of Green Emeralds. Look!

Dorothy:
What is it?

Good Witch:
(The silver shoes are sticking out from under the house). The Wicked Witch has disappeared. There is nothing left of her but her silver shoes. The silver shoes belong to you now and you must wear them from now on.

Dorothy:
But they're beautiful!

Good Witch:
There is some magic charm connected with them. She would never let them out of her sight.

Dorothy:
It's very kind of you to give them to me. I am very anxious to get back to my aunt and uncle. Can you help me find the way?

Good Witch:
You must go to the City of Emeralds and perhaps Oz will help you.

Dorothy:
Where is the City of Emeralds?

Good Witch:
It is exactly in the centre of the country, and is ruled by Oz.

Dorothy:
Is he a good man?

Good Witch:
He is a good Wizard. Whether he is a man or not, I cannot tell because I have never seen him.

Dorothy:
But how do I get there?

Good Witch:
You must walk. It is a very long journey, through a country that is sometimes dark and terrible. But you must not be afraid. I will use all the magic arts I know of to keep you from harm.

Dorothy:
Won't you come with me?

Good Witch:
No, I cannot do that, but I will give you my kiss. No one will dare injure a person who has been kissed by the Witch of the North. *(She kisses Dorothy).* You must find the way to the Emerald City by yourself, but you will find the road is paved with yellow bricks, so, you cannot miss it. When you get to the Wizard of Oz, don't be afraid of him. Tell him your story and ask him to help you. Now, I have to leave you. Don't forget, look for the yellow brick road.

Dorothy:
I wonder if the silver shoes will fit? *(She tries on the silver shoes).* Yes, they do. Now come along Toto *(Toto is her dog),* we've got a long journey in front of us. Let's look for the yellow brick road.

THE WIZARD OF OZ
by L.Frank Baum

(Dorothy meets a scarecrow who has no brains and offers to take him with her on her journey to meet the great and powerful Oz).

<u>Scarecrow:</u>
Good day.

<u>Dorothy:</u>
Did you speak?

<u>Scarecrow:</u>
Certainly, how do you do?

<u>Dorothy:</u>
I'm pretty well, thank you, how do you do?

<u>Scarecrow:</u>
I'm not feeling well for it is very tedious being perched up here night and day to scare away crows.

<u>Dorothy:</u>
Can't you get down?

<u>Scarecrow:</u>
No, for this pole is stuck up my back. If you will please take away the pole I shall be greatly obliged to you.

(Dorothy reaches up both arms and lifts the Scarecrow off the pole).

<u>Scarecrow:</u>
Thank you very much. I feel like a new man.

(The scarecrow starts to walk along beside Dorothy).

Scarecrow:
Who are you? And where are you going?

Dorothy:
My name is Dorothy and I am going to the Emerald City, to ask the great Oz to send me back to Kansas.

Scarecrow:
Where is the Emerald City and who is Oz?

Dorothy:
Why, don't you know?

Scarecrow:
No, indeed; I don't know anything. You see, I am stuffed, so I have no brains at all.

Dorothy:
Oh, I'm awfully sorry for you.

Scarecrow:
Do you think, if I go to the emerald City with you, that the great Oz would give me some brains?

Dorothy:
I cannot tell, but you may come with me, if you like. If Oz will not give you any brains you will be no worse off than you are now.

Scarecrow:
That is true. You see, I don't mind my legs and arms and body being stuffed, because I cannot get hurt. If anyone treads on my toes or sticks a pin into me, it doesn't matter, for I can't feel it. But I do not want people to call me a fool, and if my head stays stuffed with straw instead of with brains, as yours is, how am I ever to know anything?

Dorothy:
I understand how you feel. If you will come with me, I'll ask Oz to do all he can for you.
(Toto, Dorothy's dog growls at the scarecrow).
Oh, don't mind Toto, he never bites.

Scarecrow:
Oh, I'm not afraid, he can't hurt the straw. Do let me carry that basket for you. I shall not mind it, for I can't get tired. I'll tell you a secret – there is only one thing in the world I am afraid of.

Dorothy:
What's that? The Munchkin farmer who made you?

Scarecrow:
No – it's a lighted match!

THE WIZARD OF OZ
by L.Frank Baum

(Dorothy is talking to the scarecrow who has no brains. They are taking a rest on their journey towards the Emerald City).

Dorothy:
Here, scarecrow – here is some bread from my basket.

Scarecrow:
Oh, I am never hungry, and it is a lucky thing I am not. For my mouth is only painted, and if I should cut a hole in it so I could eat, the straw I am stuffed with would come out, and that would spoil the shape of my head. Tell me something about yourself, and the country you came from.

Dorothy:
Well, I come from Kansas where everything is gray and a cyclone carried me to this queer land of Oz.

Scarecrow:
I cannot understand why you should wish to leave this beautiful country and go back to the dry, gray place you call Kansas.

Dorothy:
That is because you have no brains. No matter how dreary and gray our homes are, we people of flesh and blood would rather live there than in any other country, be it ever so beautiful. There is no place like home.

Scarecrow:
(He sighs). Of course, I cannot understand it. If your heads were stuffed with straw, like mine, you would probably all live in the beautiful places, and then Kansas would have no people at all. It is fortunate for Kansas that you have brains.

Dorothy:
Won't you tell me a story, while we are resting?

Scarecrow:
My life has been so short that I really know nothing whatever. I was only made the day before yesterday. What happened in the world before that time is all unknown to me. Luckily, when the farmer made my head, one of the first things he did was to paint my ears, so that I heard what was going on. Then he painted my right eye, and as soon as it was finished, I found myself looking at him and at everything around me with a great deal of curiosity, for this was my first glimpse of the world. Then he made my second eye and I could see much better than before. Then he made my nose and my mouth; but I did not speak, because at that time, I didn't know what a mouth was for. I had fun watching him make my body and my arms and legs and when they fastened on my head, I felt very proud, for I thought I was just as good a man as anyone.

Dorothy:
You must have scared the crows away fast enough for you look just like a man.

Scarecrow:
But then the farmer took me to a cornfield and set me up on a tall stick, where you found me and left me alone. The crows told me that if I had brains in my head, I would be as good as any man. I am sure the great Oz will give me brains as soon as we get to the Emerald City.

Dorothy:
I hope so - since you seem anxious to have them.

Scarecrow:
Oh yes; I am anxious. It is such an uncomfortable feeling to know one is a fool.

Dorothy:
Well then – let us go. Here, take my basket. We need to

travel though this great forest where the trees are so big and close together that their branches meet over the road of yellow brick. Come, it's almost dark.

Scarecrow:
If this road goes in, it must come out and as the Emerald City is at the other end of the road, we must go wherever it leads us.

Dorothy:
Anyone would know that!

Scarecrow:
Certainly; that is why I know it. If it required brains to figure it out, I never should have said it.

Dorothy:
If you see any house, or any place where we can pass the night you must tell me; for it is very uncomfortable walking in the dark.

Scarecrow:
I see a little cottage at the right of us built of logs and branches. Shall we go there?

Dorothy:
Yes, indeed. I am all tired out.

THE WIZARD OF OZ
by L.Frank Baum

(Dorothy meets a tinman who has no heart. They are on their journey towards the Emerald City).

<u>Dorothy:</u>
(Dorothy hears a groan).
What was that? Let's go and see.

(There is another groan. They go towards the sound and discover a man made entirely of tin. He is standing perfectly motionless).

<u>Dorothy:</u>
Did you groan?

<u>Tinman:</u>
Yes, I did. I've been groaning for more than a year, and no one has ever heard me before or come to help me.

<u>Dorothy:</u>
What can I do for you?

<u>Tinman:</u>
Get an oil-can and oil my joints. They are rusted so badly that I cannot move them at all; if I am well-oiled I shall soon be all right again. You will find an oil-can on a shelf in my cottage.

(Dorothy runs off to the cottage and fetches the oil-can. She soon returns).

<u>Dorothy:</u>
Where are your joints?

Tinman:
Oil my neck, first. *(Dorothy does so)*. Now oil the joints in my arms. *(The tin man moves carefully until he is free from rust and as good as new)*. That is a great comfort. I have been holding that axe in the air ever since I rusted, and I'm glad to be able to put it down at last. Now, if you will oil the joints of my legs, I shall be all right once more. Thankyou. I might have stood there always if you had not come along, so you have certainly saved my life. How did you happen to be here?

Dorothy:
The scarecrow and I are on our way to the Emerald City, to see the great Oz, and we stopped at your cottage to pass the night.

Tinman:
Why do you wish to see Oz?

Dorothy:
I want him to send me back to Kansas; and the Scarecrow wants him to put a few brains into his head.

Tinman:
Do you suppose Oz could give me a heart?

Dorothy:
Why I guess so, it would be as easy as to give the Scarecrow brains.

Tinman:
True. So, if you will allow me to join your party, I will also go to the Emerald City and ask Oz to help me. Please will you take my oil-can in your basket for if I should be caught in the rain, and rust again, I would need the oil-can badly.

Dorothy:
And now Mr Tin Woodman, tell us your story.

Tinman:
I was born the son of a woman who chopped down trees in the forest and sold the wood for a living. When I grew up, I too became a wood-chopper, and after my father died I took care of my old mother as long as she lived. Then I made up my mind that instead of living alone I would marry, so that I might not become lonely. There was one of the Munchkin girls who was so beautiful that I soon grew to love her with all my heart. She, on her part, promised to marry me as soon as I could earn enough money to build a better house for her; so, I set to work harder than ever. But the girl lived with an old woman who did not want her to marry anyone, for she was so lazy she wished the girl to remain with her and do the cooking and the housework. So, the old woman went to the wicked Witch of the East and promised her two sheep and a cow if she would prevent the marriage. Thereupon the wicked Witch enchanted my axe, and when I was chopping away the axe slipped and cut off my left leg. So, I went to a tin-smith and had him make me a new leg out of tin. This angered the wicked Witch of the East and soon, my enchanted axe slipped again and cut off my right leg and then my arms and then my head. Once I was made of tin, I realized I had no heart so that I lost all my love for the Munchkin girl. No one can love who has not a heart and so I am resolved to ask Oz to give me one. If he does, I will go back to the Munchkin maiden and marry her.

Dorothy:
Then Mr Tin Woodman, you will come with us to the Emerald City and ask the great Oz for a heart!

THE WIZARD OF OZ
by L. Frank Baum

(Dorothy and her dog Toto are on their way to the Emerald City to seek the great Oz. She is with her two companions, Scarecrow and Tinman, when they come across a cowardly lion).

Dorothy:
Don't you dare to bite Toto! You ought to be ashamed of yourself, a big beast like you, to bite a poor little dog!

Lion:
I didn't bite him.

Dorothy:
No, but you tried to. You are nothing but a big coward.

Lion:
I know it, I've always known it. But how can I help it?

Dorothy:
I don't know, I'm sure. To think of your striking a stuffed man, like the poor Scarecrow!

Lion:
Is he stuffed?

Dorothy:
Of course, he's stuffed.

Lion:
That's why he went over so easily. It astonished me to see him whirl around so. Is the other one stuffed also?

Dorothy:
No, he's made of tin.

Lion:
That's why he nearly blunted my claws. When they scratched against the tin it made a cold shiver run down my back. What is that little animal you are so tender of?

Dorothy:
He is my dog, Toto.

Lion:
Is he made of tin, or stuffed?

Dorothy:
Neither. He's a – a real dog.

Lion:
Oh. He's a curious animal, and seems remarkably small, now that I look at him. No one would think of biting such a little thing except a coward like me.

Dorothy:
What makes you a coward?

Lion:
It's a mystery. I suppose I was born that way. All the other animals in the forest naturally expect me to be brave, for the Lion is everywhere thought to be the King of Beasts. I learned that if I roared very loudly every living thing was frightened and got out of my way. Whenever I've met a man, I've been awfully scared; but I just roared at him, and he has always run away as fast as he could go. If the elephants and the tigers and the bears had ever tried to fight me, I should have run myself – I'm such a coward; but just as soon as they hear me roar, they all try to get away from me, and of course I let them go.

Dorothy:
But the King of Beasts shouldn't be a coward.

Lion:
I know it, it is my great sorrow, and makes my life very unhappy.

But whenever there is danger my heart begins to beat fast.

Dorothy:
Perhaps you have heart disease. If you have, you ought to be glad, for it proves you have a heart.

Lion:
Perhaps, if I had no heart, I should not be a coward.

Dorothy:
Do you have brains?

Lion:
I suppose so. I've never looked to see.

Dorothy:
We are going to see the great Oz. Scarecrow is going to ask for a brain and Tinman is going to ask for a heart. And I am going to ask him to send Toto and me back to Kansas.

Lion:
Do you think Oz could give me some courage? If you don't mind, I'll go with you for my life is simply unbearable without a bit of courage.

Dorothy:
You will be very welcome for you will help to keep away the other wild beasts. It seems to me they must be more cowardly than you are if they allow you to scare them so easily.

Lion:
They really are – but that doesn't make me any braver, and as long as I know myself to be a coward, I shall be unhappy.

PINOCCHIO
by CARLO COLLODI

(Pinocchio returns home from his travels as he is hungry. Geppetto, Pinocchio's father, spoils him and gives Pinocchio his own breakfast).

Geppetto:
Open the door!

Pinocchio:
Dear papa, I cannot!

Geppetto:
Why can't you?

Pinocchio:
(lying). Because my feet have been eaten.

Geppetto:
And who has eaten your feet?

Pinocchio:
The cat.

Geppetto:
Open the door, I tell you! If you don't, when I get into the house you shall have the cat from me!

Pinocchio:
I cannot stand up, believe me. Oh, poor me! Poor me! I shall have to walk on my knees for the rest of my life!

(Geppetto takes pity on Pinocchio).

Geppetto:
My little Pinocchio! How did you manage to burn your feet?

Pinocchio:
I don't know, papa, but it has been such a dreadful night that I shall remember it as long as I live. It thundered and lightened, and I was very hungry, and then the Talking-Cricket said to me: 'It serves you right; you have been wicked and you deserve it' and I said to him: 'Take care, Cricket! and he said: 'You are a puppet and you have a wooden head,' and I threw the handle of a hammer at him, and he died, but the fault was his, for I didn't wish to kill him. And I returned home at once, and because I was always hungry. I put my feet on the brazier to dry them, and then you returned, and I found they were burnt off, and I am always hungry, but I have no longer any feet! Oh! Oh! Oh! Oh! (*He cries*).

Geppetto:
These three pears were intended for my breakfast, but I will give them to you willingly. Eat them, and I hope they will do you good.

Pinocchio:
If you wish me to eat them, be kind enough to peel them for me.

Geppetto:
Peel them? I should never have thought, my boy, that you were so dainty and fastidious. That is bad! In this world we should accustom ourselves from childhood to like and to eat everything, for there is no saying to what we may be brought.

Pinocchio:
You are no doubt right, but I will never eat fruit that has not been peeled. I cannot bear rind.

(*Geppetto peels the fruit for Pinocchio. When Pinocchio eats the fruit, he starts to throw away the core*).

Geppetto:
Do not throw it away; in this world everything may be of use.

Pinocchio:
But core I am determined I will not eat. I am as hungry as ever!

Geppetto:
But, my boy, I have nothing more to give you! I have only the rind and the cores of the three pears.

Pinocchio:
I must have patience! If there is nothing else, I will eat the rind. *(He suddenly realises the core and the rind does not taste so bad)*. Ah! Now I feel comfortable.

Geppetto:
You see, now, that I was right when I said to you that it did not do to accustom ourselves to be too particular or too dainty in our tastes. We can never know, my dear boy, what may happen to us.

PINOCCHIO
by CARLO COLLODI

(On his travels, Pinocchio meets a talking cricket named Jiminy Cricket).

<u>Cricket:</u>
Cri-cri-cri…

<u>Pinocchio:</u>
Who calls me? *(He is frightened).*

<u>Cricket:</u>
It is I!

<u>Pinocchio:</u>
Tell me, Cricket, who may you be?

<u>Cricket:</u>
I am the Talking-Cricket, and I have lived in this room a hundred years or more.

<u>Pinocchio:</u>
Now, however, this room is mine, and if you would do me a pleasure go away at once, without even turning round.

<u>Cricket:</u>
I will not go until I have told you a great truth.

<u>Pinocchio:</u>
Tell it me, then, and be quick about it.

<u>Cricket:</u>
Woe to those boys who rebel against their parents and run away from home. They will never come to any good in the world, and sooner or later they will repent bitterly.

Pinocchio:
Sing away, Cricket, as you please, and as long as you please. For me, I have made up my mind to run away tomorrow at daybreak, because if I remain, I shall not escape the fate of all other boys; I shall be sent to school and shall be made to study either by love or by force. To tell you in confidence, I have no wish to learn; it is much more amusing to run after butterflies, or to climb trees and to take the young birds out of their nests.

Cricket:
Poor little goose! But do you not know that in that way you will grow up a perfect donkey, and that everyone will make fun of you?

Pinocchio:
Hold your tongue, you wicked, ill-omened croaker!

Cricket:
But if you do not wish to go to school why not at least learn a trade, if only to enable you to earn honestly a piece of bread!

Pinocchio:
Do you want me to tell you? Amongst all the trades in the world there is only one that really takes my fancy.

Cricket:
And that trade – what is it?

Pinocchio:
It is to eat, drink, sleep and amuse myself, and to lead a vagabond life from morning to night.

Cricket:
As a rule, all those who follow that trade, end almost always either in a hospital or in a prison.

Pinocchio:
Take care, you wicked, ill-omened croaker! Woe to you if I fly into a passion!

Cricket:
Poor Pinocchio! I really pity you!

Pinocchio:
Why do you pity me?

Cricket:
Because you are a puppet and, what is worse, because you have a wooden head.

(Pinocchio jumps up in a rage and snatches a wooden hammer and throws it at the Talking-Cricket. The hammer strikes the cricket on the head and the Cricket is flattened against the wall).

Cricket:
Cri-cri –cri-! Cri-cri-cri! *(He dies).*

Pinocchio:
The Talking-Cricket was right. I did wrong to rebel against my papa and to run away from home. If my papa were here, I should not now be dying of yawning! Oh, what a dreadful illness hunger is!

PINOCCHIO
by CARLO COLLODI

(Pinocchio has a high fever. A Fairy approaches and gives him some white powder in half a tumbler of water. Pinocchio makes all sorts of excuses in order to get out of taking his medicine).

Fairy:
Drink it and in a few days, you will be cured.

Pinocchio:
Is it sweet or bitter?

Fairy:
It is bitter.

Pinocchio:
If it is bitter, I will not take it.

Fairy:
Drink it, and when you have drunk it, I will give you a lump of sugar to take away the taste.

Pinocchio:
Where is the lump of sugar?

Fairy:
Here it is.

Pinocchio:
Give me the lump of sugar first and then I will drink that bad, bitter water.

Fairy:
Do you promise me?

Pinocchio:
It would be a fine thing if sugar were medicine! I would take it every day.

Fairy:
Now keep your promise and drink these few drops of water, which will restore you to health.

Pinocchio:
It is too bitter! I cannot drink it.

Fairy:
How can you tell that, when you have not even tasted it?

Pinocchio:
I can imagine it! I know it from the smell. I want first another lump of sugar and then I will drink it! *(The fairy gives him another lump of sugar).* I cannot drink it so! Because that pillow that is down there on my feet bothers me.

(The fairy removes the pillow).

Fairy:
What is the matter now?

Pinocchio:
The door of the room, which is half open, bothers me (*The fairy closes the door).* I will not drink that bitter water – no, no, no!

Fairy:
My boy, you will repent it. Your illness is serious. The fever in a few hours will carry you into the other world. Are you not afraid of death?

Pinocchio:
I am not in the least afraid! I would rather die than drink that bitter medicine.

(Four ghostly black rabbits enter carrying a coffin). What do you want with me? I am not yet dead.

Fairy:
Those ghostly rabbits will take you to the after-life.

Pinocchio:
Oh, Fairy, Fairy! Give me the tumbler at once; be quick, for pity's sake, for I will not die – no, I will not die. *(Pinocchio jumps out of bed, rushing around until he realises he is not going to die).*

Fairy:
Then my medicine has really done you good?

Pinocchio:
Good? I should think so. It has restored me to life!

Fairy:
Then why on earth did you require so much persuasion to take it?

Pinocchio:
Because you see that we boys are all like that! We are more afraid of medicine than of the illness.

Fairy:
Disgraceful! Boys ought to know that a good remedy taken in time may save them from a serious illness, and perhaps even from death.

Pinocchio:
Oh! But another time I shall not require so much persuasion. I shall remember those black rabbits with the coffin on their shoulders and then I shall immediately take the tumbler in my hand, and down it will go!

TOM SAWYER
by MARK TWAIN

(Tom has the task of painting a fence for his Aunt Polly. His friend, Ben, comes along nibbling an apple. Tom finds a way to get Ben to paint the fence for him. This story is set in America).

Tom:
Why, it's you, Ben! I weren't noticing.

Ben:
Say – I'm going swimming, I am. Don't you wish you could? But of course, you'd rather work – wouldn't you? Course you would!

Tom:
What do you call work?

Ben:
Why, ain't that work?

Tom:
Well, maybe it is, and maybe it ain't. All I know, is, it suits Tom Sawyer.

Ben:
Oh come, now, you don't mean to let on that you *like* it?

Tom:
Like it? Well, I don't see why I oughtn't to like it. Does a boy get a chance to whitewash a fence every day?

(Tom continues painting. Ben watches with interest).

Ben:
Say, Tom, let *me* whitewash a little.

Tom:
No – no – I reckon it wouldn't hardly do, Ben. You see, Aunt Polly's awful particular about this fence – right here on the street, you know – but if it was the back fence I wouldn't mind and she wouldn't either. Yes, she's awful particular about this fence; it's got to be done very careful; I reckon there ain't one boy in a thousand, maybe two thousand, that can do it the way it's got to be done.

Ben:
Is that so? Oh come, now – lemme just try. Only just a little – I'd let *you*, if you was *me*, Tom.

Tom:
I'd like to, Ben, but Aunt Polly – well, Jim wanted to do it, but she wouldn't let him; Sid wanted to do it, and she wouldn't let Sid. Now don't you see how I'm fixed? If *you* was to tackle this fence and anything was to happen to it –

Ben:
Oh, shucks, I'll be just as careful. Now lemme try. Say – I'll give you the core of my apple.

Tom:
Well, here – No, Ben, now don't. I'm afeard –

(Tom gives Ben the brush with reluctance on his face but joy in his heart. Tom sits and enjoys the apple whilst Ben slaves away painting the fence).

Ben:
Ok, now I'll I give you *all* of my apple!

(Tom walks away munching the apple whilst Ben busily begins painting. His trick has worked).

PUSS IN BOOTS – A FAIRY TALE

(Puss in boots is originally from an Italian fable but is now known all over the world. A poor Miller sets out to seek his fortune with his loyal cat. The Miller's son is sitting sadly on a stump, trying to mend his ragged coat and a pair of boots).

Miller:
Oh, dear! I don't think anyone was ever so unlucky as I am. There are my two brothers finely set up, the eldest with the mill that Father left him, and the next one with the donkey; now one of them can grind all the corn that they bring him from the village, and the other can cart the meal round; but they haven't any use for *me*, because Father left me *nothing* but his cat. Of course, it's a very good-natured cat, and can talk, too, which is more than most cats can do, but I don't see how it's going to get me a living, as he said it would do. And my brothers won't even give me any new clothes – only old meal-bags to patch my coat with. Oh, dear! *(Puss bounds in, rubs against the Miller's Son)* Well, Puss, what are we going to do to earn our living?

Puss:
Is that all that is worrying you, master? Oh, we shall do well enough, never fear. Supposing we set out to seek our fortunes together?

Miller:
What, in this coat?

Puss:
H'm, there isn't much coat left, is there? Never you mind, dear master, leave everything to me, and I'll make your fortune somehow.

Miller:
Why, what can *you* do, poor Puss?

Puss:
Aha! You'll see what I can do. Just give me a bag, and a pair of boots to save my feet from thorns –

Miller:
Boots?

Puss:
Yes, there's that pair you've outgrown – you were trying to stretch them just now, but they'll never be any good to you again; just put a patch on the heel, and they'll do very well for me. And where's that meal-bag you were trying to patch your coat with? You won't be needing any more patches for it –

Miller:
What do you want it for?

Puss:
But you will patch those boots for me, won't you, master? *(He takes the bag & exits)*

Miller:
(Mending as he talks). I wonder what Puss wants with that bag? He usually seems to know what he's about. Perhaps Father was right when he said he was leaving me something better than either of my brothers would get. I wonder.

(Puss comes back with his bag full of rabbits).

Hullo! What have you got there?

Puss:

Rabbits, nice plump young rabbits. I snared them as they were playing outside their burrows. Have you mended that hole, master? (*Miller's son hands him the boots & he puts them on*) Oh, well done! – I couldn't have made a better job of it myself. *(Strutting)* What do you think of me now, master?

Miller:

(Laughing). Puss in boots! *(He seizes his paws and they dance around together).*

Puss:

(swaggering). Puss in boots! Ha! Ha! Puss in Boots, servant to the Miller's son – but you shall have a grander name than that soon!

Miller:

What do you mean?

Puss:

Just leave it all to me. And now, how about setting out to see the world?

Miller:

Yes, let's set out to see the world!

(Pause to allow the passing of time as they set off to see the world. Or their journey could be acted out in mime).

Puss:

Which way shall we go – through the forest or down to the sea?

Miller:

I rather like the look of those hills with the castle under them.

Puss:

Do you know who lives there?

Miller:
No – who?

Puss:
An ogre.

Miller:
An ogre?

Puss:
He's a magician too – or so I've heard.

Miller:
Really and truly?

Puss:
All these lands are his –

Miller:
Hush! Don't you hear someone coming? Along the road there?

Puss:
We'll lie hidden here until we see who it is. Don't move – they are coming round the corner.

Miller:
Why, it's the royal coach – and the King himself inside – and the Princess, too – how lovely she is!

Puss:

Master, I've got a plan! Don't stir – not so much as a finger or toe – until I tell you.

(Puss approaches the King, bowing.)

Your Majesty, pardon me for delaying your royal progress – but I was sent by my master, the – the Marquis of Carabbas, to offer you tribute from his lands, over which you are now driving. Your Majesty, I left him just now bathing in one of his lakes, not far from here. Shall I summon him to your presence?

(Puss exits. Pause). Help! Help! *(Re-Appearing).*

Oh, my poor master! A dreadful accident has just happened to my master, your Majesty! He was set upon while he was bathing, by some brigands, desperate fellows – they tried to drown him! I beat them off, twenty or thirty of them, but I could not prevent them from carrying away all his clothes.

You have more in the coach, your Majesty? *(Puss takes a bundle of fine clothes from the King, bowing as he leaves).* He will soon be ready to thank your Majesty.

(Puss exits and soon returns with the Miller. He introduces his master as the Marquis).

Your Majesty, my master, the Marquis of Carabbas.

Miller://
(Bowing to the King). Your Majesty, I am honoured.

Puss:

(To his master). You won't forget to leave orders with me about the harvest, will you, master?

Miller:

(Astonished). What harvest?

Puss:

Hush! Now, as you go along persuade the King to stop whenever he passes any reapers and ask them who their master is.

Miller:
Why?

Puss:

Because I am going to run ahead of you and tell them how to answer. And when you get to the castle, stop the coach and knock at the door –

Miller:

Knock at the ogre's door? What are you thinking, Puss?

Puss:

Never mind – the King is waiting – only do just as I tell you, dear master, and all will be well.

TOAD OF TOAD HALL
by A.A. Milne
Adapted from Wind in the Willows
by Kenneth Grahame

(This is the opening scene is from Act One. Marigold is on the telephone to Mr Rat. Her nurse overhears her conversation. Marigold tells her nurse that she has met the creatures from the riverbank).

Marigold:
Hallo, is that the Exchange? I want River Bank 1001 ... Hallo, is that the Water Rat's house? ... Oh, I beg your pardon. They've given me the wrong number. I wanted Mr Rat's house and you've given me Mr Badger's. *(To herself)* Sorry you've been troubled ... Hallo, is that the Water Rat's house? Is that Mr Rat speaking? Good morning, Mr Rat, this is Marigold speaking ... Yes, isn't it a delightful day? ... Yes. Well, almost alone. Nurse is here, but she's asleep. How's Mr Mole? ... Oh, haven't you seen him? I expect he's very busy spring-cleaning. You see, when your house is all basement, there's such a lot of spring-cleaning to be done ... Yes, I prefer a riverside residence too ... May I really come one day? How lovely ... No, not tomorrow, I'm having tea with Mr Toad ... Yes, conceited, but so nice ... I saw Mr Otter just now, just before I rang up ... No, I don't know him very well, but I think he's sweet ... Will you really? And if Mr Mole – Oh, Nurse is awake. Goodbye.

Nurse:
Well, really, Marigold, you do think of funny things.

Marigold:
(She puts down the telephone). Have you been overhearing, Nurse?

Nurse:
Couldn't help it, dearie, you're that funny – with your Mr Rat and Mr Toad and all, just as if they were human beings.

Marigold:
But so they are.

Nurse:
Human beings? *(surprised)*.

Marigold:
Yes. I mean they are as human to themselves as – as we are to us.

Nurse:
No, it's no good, dearie, I can't follow it.

Marigold:
I mean, they must *seem* quite big and grown up and human to each other.

Nurse:
Now fancy that!

Marigold:
Mr Toad, he's all puffed out and conceited, but very nice, you know, and very sorry afterwards for talking so much about himself. And Mr Rat's a dear – that's him I was talking to just now. He's very quick and clever and helpful, and his little sharp eyes are always looking out so as to see that he doesn't hurt people's feelings. And Mr Mole – I'm not sure about him. You see, he loves the underground a good deal, and doesn't go out into society much, so I should think he'd be rather simple, and not liking to talk about himself, and just saying 'Yes' and 'No', and waiting to be asked before he has a second cup. And then Mr Badger – of course he's grey, and much older than the others, and very fatherly – and sleeps a good deal with a handkerchief over his face, and says 'Now, now, now' and 'Well, well, well' when he's woken up.

Nurse:
Well, well, well, fancy that now! Why, you might almost have seen them at it, the way you talk.

Marigold:
I have seen them.

Nurse:
Never!

Marigold:
One morning. I came out here early, oh, ever so early. Nobody was up – you weren't up, and the birds weren't up, and even the sun wasn't up – and everything was so still that there was no sound in all the world, except just the wind in the willows, whispering ever so gently.

Nurse:
What your poor mother would have said – *(suddenly showing interest)*. Well, and what happened?

Marigold:
I don't know. I sat there and waited for everything to wake up, and then by and by I heard something – music, very thin and clear and far off – and then – well, then there was the sun, and it was daylight, and it seemed as if I had just woken up myself. I've never really seen them since. I pretend to talk to them, just as if they were really there, but – Wouldn't it be lovely if they suddenly came out and began to talk – Mole from under the ground there, and the Water Rat from his hole in the bank, and the old Badger from the dead leaves in the ditch, and Mr Toad. Oh, Nurse, wouldn't it be lovely?

Nurse:
I should be that frightened, if they were all big.

Marigold:
Oh, no, you wouldn't, because they wouldn't know we were here. We should just listen to them, without their knowing anything about it. Mr Mole! Mr Rat! Mr Toad! Oh, Nurse, wouldn't it be lovely?

Nurse:
Ooh, I can hear something! Listen!

Marigold:
That's the music again. Quick! Hide!

TOAD OF TOAD HALL
by A.A. Milne
Adapted from Wind in the Willows
by Kenneth Grahame

(Rat lives on the riverbank. He is talking to his new friend, Mole, about the joys of living on the riverbank).

<u>Rat:</u>
Hallo Mole! Don't seem to have seen you about before.

<u>Mole:</u>
I – I don't go out much, as a rule.

<u>Rat:</u>
Prefer home-life? I know. Very good thing too in its way.

<u>Mole:</u>
Yes, you see, I – This is a river, isn't it?

<u>Rat:</u>
This is *the* river.

<u>Mole:</u>
I've never seen a river before.

<u>Rat:</u>
Never seen a – You never – Well, I – what *have* you been doing then?

<u>Mole:</u>
Is it as nice as that?

Rat:
Nice? My dear young friend, believe me, it's the *only* thing. There is *nothing* – absolutely nothing – half so much worth doing as simply messing – messing about by a river – or *in* a river – or *on* a river. It doesn't matter which.

Mole:
But what do *you* do?

Rat:
Do? Nothing. Just mess about. That's the charm of it; you're always busy, and yet you never do anything in particular; and when you've done it, there's always something else to do, and you can do it if you like, but you'd much better not ... And so, you've never *seen* a river before? Well, well!

Mole:
Never. And you actually live by it? What a jolly life it sounds.

Rat:
I live by it, and with it and on it and in it. It's brother and sister to me, and aunts and company, and food and drink, and naturally – washing. It's my world, and I don't want any other.

Mole:
Isn't it a bit dull at times? Just you and the river and no one else to pass a word with?

Rat:
No one else to – no one – Oh well, I mustn't be hard on you. You are new to it. But believe me, my dear young friend, the Riverbank is so crowded nowadays that many people are moving away altogether. Otters, kingfishers, dabchicks, moorhens – No one else to – Oh, my dear young friend!

Mole:

I am afraid you must think me very ignorant.

Rat:

Not at all. Naturally, not being used to it. Look here, what are you doing today?

Mole:

I – I was spring-cleaning.

Rat:

On a day like this!

Mole:

That's just it. Sometimes I seem to hear a voice within me say 'Whitewash', and then another voice says 'Hang whitewash'! And I don't quite know which of the – I don't quite know – I don't quite – Oh, hang whitewash!

Rat:

That's the spirit! Well, what I was about to suggest was a trifle of lunch on the bank here, and then I'd take you round and introduce you to a few of my friends. Does that appeal to you at all?

Mole:

Does that appeal to me? Does it? Oh my, oh my, oh my!

Rat:

There, there! You don't want to get *too* excited. It's only just a trifle of lunch. Cold tongue – cold ham – cold chicken – salad – French rolls – cress sandwiches – hard-boiled eggs – bloater paste – tinned peaches – meringues – ginger beer – lemonade – milk – chocolate – oranges – Nothing special – only just –

Mole:

Stop, stop! Oh my, oh my! Oh, what a day!

Rat:

That's all right. You'll feel better soon. Now just you wait here – don't go falling into the river or anything like that – and I'll be back in two minutes with the luncheon-basket.

Mole:

Oh, Mr Rat, my generous friend, I – I – words fail me for the moment– I – your kindness – that expression, if I caught it correctly, 'luncheon-basket' – a comparative stranger like myself – did I hear you say 'bloater paste?' – you – I – Oh, what a day! I want to stay with you. And – learn about your river.

TOAD OF TOAD HALL
by A.A. Milne
Adapted from Wind in the Willows
by Kenneth Grahame

(The Wild Wood. Mole is terrified in the wild wood until Ratty comes to the rescue).

Mole:

(Hopefully) Ratty! *(in a sudden panic)* What's that? *(The movement stops).* Pooh! It's nothing! I'm not frightened! ... I do wish Ratty were here. He's so comforting, is Ratty. Or the brave Mr Toad. He'd frighten them all away. *(He hears the sound of mocking laughter).* What's that? *(He looks around anxiously).* Ratty always said, 'Don't go into the Wild Wood.' That's what he always said. 'Not by yourself,' he said. 'It isn't safe,' he said. 'We never do,' he said. That's what Ratty said. But I thought I knew better. There he was, dear old Rat, dozing in front of the fire, and I thought if I just slipped out, just to see what the Wild Wood was like – *(He breaks off suddenly and darts round, fearing an attack from behind. There is nothing).* I should be safer up against a tree. Why didn't I think of that before? *(He settles himself at the foot of a tree).* Ratty would have thought of it, he's so wise. Oh, Ratty, I wish you were here! It's so much more friendly with two!

Rat:

Moly! Moly! Moly! Where are you? It's me – it's old Rat!

Mole:

(He hears a voice from far off). What's that? Who is it?

(Rat appears; a lantern in his hand, a couple of pistols in his belt, and a cudgel over his shoulder).

Rat:
There, there!

Mole:
Oh, Rat! Oh, Rat! Oh, Ratty, I've been so frightened, you can't think!

Rat:
I know, I know. You shouldn't have gone and done it, Mole. I did my best to keep you from it. We River-Bankers hardly ever come, except in couples.

Mole:
You've come by yourself. That's because you're so brave.

Rat:
It isn't just bravery, it's knowing. There are a hundred things you have to know, which we understand about, and you don't as yet. I mean passwords and signs, and sayings which have power and effect, and plants you carry in your pocket, and verse you repeat backwards, and dodges and tricks you practise; all simple enough if you know them, but if you don't, you'll find yourself in trouble. Of course, if you're Badger, it's different.

Mole:
Surely the brave Mr Toad wouldn't mind coming here by himself?

Rat:
Old Toad? He wouldn't show his face here alone, for a whole hatful of guineas, Toad wouldn't.

Mole:
Oh, Rat! It is comforting to hear somebody laugh again.

Rat:
Poor old Mole! What a rotten time you've had. Never mind, we'll soon be home now. How would a little mulled ale strike you - after you've got into slippers, of course? I made the fire up specially.

Mole:
You think of everything, Ratty.

Rat:
Well, shall we start?

Mole:
Oh, Ratty. I don't know how to tell you, and I'm afraid you'll never want me for a companion again - but I can't, I simply can't go all that way now. I'm tired. I'm aching all over. Oh, Ratty, do forgive me. I feel as if I must just sit here for ever and ever and ever, and I'm not a bit frightened now you're with me – and – and I think I want to go to sleep.

Rat:
That's all right. But we can't stop here. Suppose we go and dig in that mound there and see if we can't make some sort of a shelter out of the snow and the wind and have a good rest. And then start for home a bit later on. How's that?

Mole:
Just as you like.

Rat:
Come on then.

(Rat leads the way and Mole trips suddenly).

Mole:
Oh, my leg! Oh, my poor shin! Ow! Ow!

<u>Rat:</u>
Poor old Mole, you don't seem to be having much luck today.

<u>Mole:</u>
I must have tripped over a stump or something. Oh my! Oh my!

<u>Rat:</u>
It's a very clean cut. That was never done by a stump. Looks like the sharp edge of something metal. Funny!

<u>Mole:</u>
Well, never mind what's done it. It hurts just the same whatever's done it.

<u>Rat:</u>
Wait a moment. (*He begins scratching at the snow*).

<u>Mole:</u>
What is it?

<u>Rat:</u>
I thought so!

<u>Mole:</u>
What is it?

<u>Rat:</u>
Come and see.

<u>Mole:</u>
Hullo, a door-scraper! How very careless of somebody!

<u>Rat:</u>
But don't you see what it means?

Mole:
Of course, I see what it means. It means that some very forgetful person has left his door-scraper lying about in the middle of the Wild Wood just where it's sure to trip everybody up. Somebody ought to write to him about it.

Rat:
Oh, Mole, how stupid you are. There! What's that?

Mole:
It looks like a door-mat.

Rat:
It *is* a door-mat. And what does that tell you?

Mole:
Nothing, Rat, nothing. Who ever heard of a door-mat telling anyone anything? They simply don't do it. They are not that sort at all. What have you found now?

Rat:
There!
(*He fetches the lantern and holds it up to the nameplate*).
What do you read there?

Mole:
'Mr Badger. Seventh Wednesdays'... Rat!

Rat:
What do you think of that?

Mole:
Rat, you're a wonder, that's what you are! I see it all now. *You* argued it out step by step from the moment when I fell and cut my shin, and you looked at the cut, and your majestic mind said to itself, 'Door-scraper'. Did it stop there? No. Your powerful brain said to itself, 'Where there's a scraper, there must be a mat.

Rat:
Quite so.

Mole:
'I have noticed before,' said the wise Mr Rat,' That where there's a scraper there must be a mat'. And did you stop there? NO! Your intellect still went on working. It said grandly to itself, 'Where there's a door-mat there must be a door.'

Rat:
I suppose you are going to sit on the snow and talk all night. Now wake up a bit and hang on to this bell-pull, while I hammer.

Mole:
(*Sleepily*). Oh, all right!

TOAD OF TOAD HALL
by A.A. Milne
Adapted from Wind in the Willows
by Kenneth Grahame

(Rat and Mole have just left Badger's house where they have been discussing what they are going to do about Toad. Mole compares his own humble abode to the homes of his other friends).

Rat:
Talking to Toad will never cure him. He'll say anything.

Mole:
Yes.

Rat:
We must do something. What's the matter, old fellow? You seem melancholy. Too much beef?

Mole:
Oh, no, it isn't that. It was just – no, never mind, I shall be all right directly.

Rat:
Why, whatever is it?

Mole:
Nothing, Ratty, nothing. I was just admiring Badger's great big house and comparing it with my own little home, which – which I haven't seen lately – just comparing it, you know, and thinking about it – and thinking about it – and comparing it. Not meaning to, you know. Just happening to – think about it.

Rat:
Oh, Mole!

Mole:
I know it's a shabby, dingy little place; not like your cosy quarters, or Toad's beautiful Hall, or Badger's great house – but it was my own little home – and I was fond of it – and I went away and forgot all about it – and since we've been down here it's all been coming back to me – perhaps it's the pickles – I always had Military Pickles too – I shall be better soon – I don't know what you'll think of me.

Rat:
Poor old Mole! Been rather an exciting day, hasn't it? And then the same sort of pickles. Tell me about Mole End. We might go and pay it a visit tomorrow if you've nothing better to do.

Mole:
It wouldn't be fine enough for you. You're used to great big places and fine houses. I noticed directly we came in how you stood with your back to the fire so grandly and easily, just as if it were nothing to you.

Rat:
Well, you tucked into the beef, old chap.

Mole:
Did I?

Rat:
Rather! Made yourself quite at home. I said to myself at once, 'Mole is used to going out,' I said. 'Weekend parties at big country houses,' I said, 'that's nothing to Mole,' I said.

Mole:
Did you really, Ratty?

Rat:
Oh, rather! Spotted it at once.

Mole:
Of course, there were features about Mole End which made it rather— rather —

Rat:
Rather a feature?

Mole:
Yes. The statuary. I'd picked up a bit of statuary here and there — you'd hardly think how it livened the place up. Garibaldi, the Infant Samuel, and Queen Victoria — dotted about in odd corners. It had a very pleasing effect, my friends used to tell me.

Rat:
I should like to have seen that, Mole, I should indeed. That must have been very striking.

Mole:
It was just about now that they used to come carol-singing.

Rat:
Garibaldi — and the others?

Mole:
The field-mice.

Rat:
Oh yes, of course.

Mole:
Quite an institution they were. They never passed me over — always came to Mole End last, and I gave them hot drinks, and supper sometimes, when I could afford it.

Rat:
Yes, I remember now hearing about it, and what a fine place Mole End was.

Mole:
Did you? ... It wasn't very big.

Rat:
Between ourselves, I don't much care about these big places. Cosy and tasteful, that's what I always heard about Mole End.

Mole:
You're a good friend, Ratty. I like being with you.

TOAD OF TOAD HALL
by A.A. Milne
*Adapted from Wind in the Willows
by Kenneth Grahame*

(Toad is in jail for stealing a motor-car. Phoebe, the Jailer's daughter, brings him his breakfast).

Phoebe:
Good Morning, Toad.

Toad:
Good Morning, woman.

Phoebe:
Slept well?

Toad
How could I sleep well, immured in a dark and noisy dungeon like this?

Phoebe:
Well, some do ... See, I've brought your breakfast.

Toad:
This is the end. The end of everything. How can I ever be set at large again who have been imprisoned so unjustly for stealing so handsome a motor-car in such an audacious manner. Now I must languish in this dungeon till people who were proud to say they knew me have forgotten the very name of Toad.

Phoebe:
Nice hot buttered toast and tea.

Toad:
Did you say HOT buttered?

Phoebe:
Made it myself, I did. Father said, 'Here's the key of No. 87, and you can take him his breakfast. He's the most dangerous animal in the country and how we shall keep him under lock and key goodness only knows – '

Toad:
Did he say that?

Phoebe:
His very words. And you can take him a couple of old crusts for his breakfast, because I must starve and break his indomitable spirit. So I said, 'Yes, Father,' and as soon as his back was turned I made this nice buttered toast.

Toad:
I am not ungrateful. You must pay me a visit at Toad Hall one of these days. Drop in for tea one afternoon.

Phoebe:
Is that where you live?

Toad:
Finest house in these parts for miles around.

Phoebe:
Tell me about it.

Toad:
Toad Hall is an eligible, self-contained gentleman's residence, very unique.

Phoebe:
Fancy! And do your friends Mr Badger and Mr Rat and Mr Mole live there with you?

Toad:
Oh, my dear child! Badger! Rat! Mole! They come to pay me a visit now and then. but well, quite frankly, they wouldn't be comfortable at a big house like Toad Hall, not to live.

Phoebe:
You're feeling better, aren't you?

Toad:
We have our ups and downs. Any prisoners ever been known to escape from this castle of yours?

Phoebe:
Never. But I think I see a way in which you might escape.

Toad:
You're going to help me?

Phoebe:
Yes. I like you, Toad. I have an aunt who is a washerwoman.

Toad:
I have several aunts who *ought* to be washerwomen.

Phoebe:
Do be quiet a minute, Toad. Now my aunt does the washing for all the prisoners in the castle. She brings the washing back Friday mornings – that's today. Now you're very rich and for a few pounds I think I could persuade her to lend you her dress and bonnet and you could escape as the castle washerwoman. You're very much alike in some ways – Particularly about the figure.

Toad:
We're *not*! I have a very elegant figure – for what I am.

Phoebe:
So has my aunt. You are a horrid, proud, ungrateful animal - when I'm trying to help you!

Toad:
You surely wouldn't have Mr. Toad, of Toad Hall, going about the country disguised as a washerwoman?

Phoebe:
Then you can stop here as a Toad. I suppose you want to go off in a coach and four horses?

Toad:
No, no! Please! You are a good, kind, clever girl, and I am indeed a proud and stupid Toad. Introduce me to your worthy aunt, if you will be so kind.

Phoebe:
That's better. With a little trouble you'd make quite a nice Toad.

TOAD OF TOAD HALL
by A.A. Milne
Adapted from Wind in the Willows
by Kenneth Grahame

(Act 4. Rat's riverside residence. Toad appears dressed as a washer woman. He has escaped from prison).

Toad:
Help! Help!

Rat:
Funny! That sounded like Toad's voice.

Toad:
Help!

Rat:
Yes, if Toad had been anywhere but where he is in prison, poor unfortunate animal, I should have said –

Toad:
Help! Help!

Rat:
It is! Toady! However …

Toad:
Give us a hand, Rat. I'm about done.

(Rat helps pull Toad into his boat).

Rat:
Come on the sofa a bit, won't you?

Toad:
Thank you, dear Ratty, thank you.

Rat:
Here drink this. You're about done. *(He hands him a bottle of ginger-beer).*

Toad:
Ah! That's better. I shall soon be all right.

Rat:
Poor old Toady! And am I wrong, or are you disguised in parts as a washerwoman who has seen better days? Escaped? In disguise? We'll soon have you all right.

Toad:
It takes a good deal to put me out, Ratty. Just a passing faintness which might happen to anyone who had been what I've been through.

Rat:
You've been through a lot, I expect.

Toad:
My dear Ratty, the times I've been through since I saw you last, you simply can't think!

Rat:
Yes. Well, when you've got those horrible things off, and cleaned yourself up a bit –

Toad:
The times! Such trials, such sufferings, and all so nobly borne!

Rat:
You'll find some dry clothes in there.

Toad:
Such escapes, such disguises, such subterfuges, and all so cleverly planned and carried out!

Rat:
Quite so.

Toad:
Been in prison – got out of it, of course! Stole a horse – rode away on it. Humbugged everybody – made 'em do exactly as I wanted. Oh, I am a smart Toad, and no mistake. Now, what do you think my very last exploit was?

Rat:
I don't know, Toad. But seeing where it was I found you, and the state you were in, I should say that somebody had dropped you into a river, and then thrown mud at you. It isn't a thing to boast about, really it isn't, Toad.

Toad:
Pooh, that was nothing. I just happened to be – to be heading a pursuit – on my horse – right in front of everybody else, in my usual way – and accidentally, not noticing the river in the enthusiasm of the chase – and the horse stopping a moment or two before I did –

Rat:
Toad! Toad! Go at once and see if you can possibly make yourself look like a respectable animal again, for a more shabby, bedraggled, disreputable-looking object than you are now, I never set eyes on. Now stop swaggering and arguing and be off. Badger and Mole will be in directly –

Toad:
Ah, yes, of course, the Mole and the badger. What's become of them, the dear fellows? I had forgotten all about them.

Rat:
You will hear in good time. Badger himself may prefer to break the news to you. Be off now, and prepare yourself – why, what's the matter?

Toad:
(Looking at himself in a mirror). Is this glass of yours all right?

Rat:
Of course. Why?

<u>Toad:</u>
You see, it's the first time I – you're quite right, Ratty. Nobody could carry off a costume like this. I'll go and change.

WINNIE THE POOH
by A.A. MILNE

(Winnie the Pooh takes a trip to Rabbit's house).

Pooh:
Rabbit? Is anybody home? What I said was, "Is anybody home?"

Rabbit:
No!

Pooh:
Bother! Isn't there anybody at all?

Rabbit:
Nobody!

Pooh:
There must be somebody there – because somebody said "nobody" – Hello. Could you kindly tell me where Rabbit is?

Rabbit:
He's gone to see his friend, Pooh Bear.

Pooh:
But this is me! Pooh.

Rabbit:
Oh well, then – come in. It IS you. I'm glad.

Pooh:
Who did you think it was?

Rabbit:
Well, you know how it is lately – you can't be too careful – can't have just anybody coming in…

Pooh:
Piglet's got to be rescued from Kanga. And I can't seem to do it alone. So, if you'll come with me –

Rabbit:
Right now?

Pooh:
You DO like to take action, don't you?

Rabbit:
Certainly!

Pooh:
Owl and Eeyore won't do anything. They're afraid of her –

Rabbit:
A-ha!

Pooh:
Not like YOU –

Rabbit:
Not at all!

Pooh:
So, let's go right now.

Rabbit:
Ah – Pooh?

Pooh:
We don't want to waste time –

Rabbit:
Wait a moment. I nearly forgot –

Pooh:
What?

Rabbit:
Lunch.

Pooh:
No time for that –

Rabbit:
Imagine my forgetting to eat lunch. Won't you join me?

Pooh:
No, no!

Rabbit:
Fancy – I didn't know I had all this honey.

Pooh:
But Piglet –

Rabbit:
Nearly a full pot, wouldn't you say?

Pooh:
Honey…

Rabbit:
Help yourself. Or would you prefer marmalade?

Pooh:
Both!

Rabbit:
Here we are.

Pooh:
I really shouldn't – take the time – must rescue Piglet.

Rabbit:
One does better at rescuing after a bite to eat.

Pooh:
Much better.

Rabbit:
One needs strength.

Pooh:
I DO feel stronger! And now.

Rabbit:
Have some more.

Pooh:
There isn't any more.

Rabbit:
I have another, someplace.

Pooh:
No, thank you – I really couldn't.

Rabbit:
Just a nibble?

WINNIE THE POOH
by A.A Milne

(Kanga and Roo have recently moved to the wood. Kanga is a very fussy mother and is over-protective of her baby, Roo. Kanga is always fussing and cleaning. Roo, on the other hand, just wants to make friends).

Kanga:
Well! Disgraceful! Perfectly disgraceful!

Roo:
Mama, can I go play with them?

Kanga:
Certainly not!

Roo:
But you said when we came to the forest, I'd have some-one to play with. And I haven't seen anybody but them. Maybe nobody else lives here!

Kanga:
Nonsense. There are plenty of animals in the forest.

Roo:
Then, where are they?

Kanga:
I simply can't understand it. But never mind – you wouldn't want to play with those two filthy creatures –

Roo:
Well …

Kanga:
Looking as if they never had a bath in their lives!

79

Roo:
Darn it!

Kanga:
(shocked). What did you say?

Roo:
Nothing.

Kanga:
I heard it, Roo. And you know what that means. When our mouth says ugly things, we must wash it. Mustn't we, Roo! There we are – My goodness, what did you do to your knee? A nasty scratch, dear. We'll have to put something on it.

Roo:
(Roo cries out in pain). Wow-w-w....

Kanga:
We don't want to get it infected, do we?

Roo:
Not IODINE! Not ...

Kanga:
Just a touch –

Roo:
Ouch!

Kanga:
There's a brave little Roo. Think how lucky you are. You wouldn't want to be like *those* creatures – with no one to look after you properly. Aren't you thankful?

Roo:
I am thankful!

Kanga:
What was that? *(She spots Piglet).*
If only something could be done for them. If I could just get hold of them for one day –

Roo:
Would they have a bath?

Kanga:
Plenty of soap and good hot water –

Roo:
Then could I play with them?

Kanga:
After a touch of disinfectant powder.

Roo:
Would they have oatmeal for breakfast?

Kanga:
And a big spoonful of Strengthening Medicine – Oh, the things I could do with them!

Roo:
Would they be thankful, too?

Kanga:
Perhaps not at first. Not right away. But no use thinking about it. I couldn't take care of all the animals in the forest, wherever they are!

Roo:
How about just one?

Kanga:
Dear, little Roo – we'll see.

Roo:
One that's my own size. It would be so nice.

Kanga:
Maybe we can arrange for you to have a playmate. I think this will do nicely.

Roo:
What will?

Kanga:
This place. For our new home.

Roo:
Are we going to live here?

Kanga:
Let's see … It has shade – privacy – plenty of water in that stream…

Roo:
Here's a caterpillar!

Kanga:
Goodness, don't touch! If you touch it, you'll need a bath. And there's so much to do, what with sweeping this place out – and getting settled –

Roo:
Mama –

Kanga:
Don't bother me now, dear.

Roo:
Somebody's coming!

Kanga:
Really?

Roo:
I hear them – and that means somebody lives in the forest!

Kanga:
Then stay near me, Roo.

Roo:
What?

Kanga:
One must be patient, and explain everything … Because if they *see* you, they'll *know* we live here. And if they know we *live* here, I shall have to invite them to tea. And, I don't want to have company yet, because everything is a mess!

PETER PAN
by J. M BARRIE

(Peter Pan has flown in through the window of the Darling family's house. He is crying and Wendy tries to comfort him. She mends his broken shadow and Peter asks her to go with him to Neverland to meet the Lost Boys).

<u>Wendy</u>:
Boy, why are you crying?

<u>Peter</u>:
I'm not crying. What is your name?

<u>Wendy</u>:
Wendy Moira Angela Darling. What is yours?

<u>Peter</u>:
Peter Pan.

<u>Wendy</u>:
Where do you live?

<u>Peter</u>:
Second to the right and then straight on till morning.

<u>Wendy</u>:
What a funny address!

<u>Peter</u>:
No, it isn't.

<u>Wendy</u>:
Peter!

<u>Peter</u>:
You mustn't touch me.

Wendy:
Why?

Peter:
No one must ever touch me.

Wendy:
Why?

Peter:
I don't know.

Wendy:
No wonder you were crying.

Peter:
I wasn't crying. But I can't get my shadow to stick on.

Wendy:
It has come off! How awful. Peter, you have been trying to stick it on with soap! It should be sewn on.

Peter:
What is 'sewn'?

Wendy:
I will sew it on for you, my little man. But we must have more light. I daresay it will hurt a little.

Peter:
I never cry. *(Peter tests out his shadow).*

Wendy:
Perhaps I should have ironed it.

Peter:
(dancing & crowing like a cockerel) Wendy, look! Oh, the cleverness of me!

<u>Wendy</u>:
You're a conceited boy. Of course, I did nothing!

<u>Peter</u>:
I can't help crowing when I'm pleased with myself. One girl is worth more than twenty boys.

<u>Wendy</u>:
Peter, how old are you?

<u>Peter</u>:
I don't know, but quite young, Wendy. I ran away the day I was born.

<u>Wendy</u>:
Ran away, why?

<u>Peter</u>:
Because I heard Father and Mother talking of what I was to be when I became a man. I want always to be a little boy and to have fun; so, I ran away to Kensington Gardens and lived a long time among the fairies.

<u>Wendy</u>:
You know fairies, Peter!

<u>Peter</u>:
One came with me. I can't think where she has gone. Tinker Bell, Tink, where are you?

<u>Wendy</u>:
Peter, you don't mean to tell me that there is a fairy in this room!

<u>Peter</u>:
You don't hear anything, do you?

<u>Wendy</u>:
I hear – the only sound I hear is like a tinkle of bells. *(Wendy can hear Tinkerbell, Peter's fairy).*

Peter:
That is the fairy language.

Wendy:
It seems to come from over there.

Peter:
Wendy, I believe I shut her up in that drawer! *(He releases Tinkerbell, who is very angry).* I'm very sorry, but how could I know you were in the drawer?

Wendy:
Oh, Peter, if only she would stand still and let me see her!

Peter:
Fairies hardly ever stand still.

Wendy:
I see her, the lovely! Where is she now?

Peter:
Tink, this lady wishes you were her fairy.

Wendy:
What does she say?

Peter:
She is not very polite. She says you are a great ugly girl, and that she is *my* fairy. She is quite a common girl, you know. She is called Tinker Bell because she mends the fairy pots and kettles.

Wendy:
Peter, where do you live?

Peter:
With the lost boys. They are the children who fall out of their

prams when the nurse is looking the other way. If they are not claimed in seven days, they are sent far away to Never Land. I'm Captain.

<u>Wendy</u>:
What fun it must be.

<u>Peter:</u>
Yes, but we are rather lonely. We have no female companionship.

<u>Wendy</u>:
Peter, why did you come to our nursery window?

<u>Peter:</u>
To hear stories. Your mother was telling you such a lovely story.

<u>Wendy</u>:
That was 'Cinderella', Peter. Where are you going?

<u>Peter:</u>
To tell the other boys.

<u>Wendy:</u>
Don't go, Peter. I know lots of stories.

<u>Peter:</u>
Come on! We'll fly.

<u>Wendy</u>:
Fly? You can fly!

<u>Peter:</u>
Wendy, come with me.

<u>Wendy</u>:
Oh dear, I mustn't. Think of Mother. Besides, I can't fly.

<u>Peter</u>:
I'll teach you.

<u>Wendy</u>:
How lovely to fly!

(They fly off through the window together, holding hands).

BEAUTY AND THE BEAST
by NICHOLAS STUART GRAY

(Beauty's two sisters, Jessamine and Jonquiline, are upset that Beauty has to return to the Beast's castle. They try to think of a way to make her stay).

Jessamine:
If we weren't quite so silly, we could think of the right things to say that would keep Beauty here with us.

Jonquiline:
We've said everything we can think of. We've begged and begged her to stay ... and oh, how we've cried.

Jessamine:
She's made up her mind.

Jonquiline:
And she's going to leave us, again.

Jessamine:
And go back to that horrid Beast, and his great dark castle. She can't like the Beast as much as she likes us.

Jonquiline:
How could she?

Jessamine:
She's sorry for him. All this week she has been worrying about him ... and wondering if he is having proper meals, and staying out at night in the forest.

Jonquiline:
I'm a bit sorry for him too, but not if he takes Beauty away from us.

Jessamine:
And he is. We can't stop her.

Jonquiline:
I hate the Beast!

Jessamine:
It's not proper to hate, Jonquiline.

Jonquiline:
I don't care. I hate him.

Jessamine:
So, do I.

Jonquiline:
I wish his horrid rose would die. It smells so sweet. Yet I wish it would die.

Jessamine:
Then the Beast would die, also.

Jonquiline:
Then … then … oh, dear, I wish we could steal the ring.

Jessamine:
Then Beauty couldn't go back to him, at all.

Jonquiline:
(She goes to the dressing table and looks at the ring).
Shall we steal it? Here it is, jessamine.

Jessamine:
That would be most improper of us, Jonquiline.

<u>Jonquiline</u>:
It would keep Beauty here with us.

<u>Jessamine:</u>
And the Beast would die.

<u>Jonquiline</u>:
Then I suppose we mustn't steal it … and Beauty must leave us. Oh, I do hate the Beast and his rose and this ring! *(She carelessly drops the ring).*

<u>Jessamine:</u>
 Oh, be careful!

<u>Jonquiline</u>:
 I don't care! I don't care! I hope it's lost! I want Beauty!

<u>Jessamine:</u>
But where has it gone? Jonquiline, help me …. I can't find the ring!

<u>Jonquiline</u>:
I don't ca … what did you say?

<u>Jessamine:</u>
I can*not* find the ring!

<u>Jonquiline</u>:
Oh, my goodness!

<u>Jessamine:</u>
Oh, be quick! It's nearly ten o'clock.

<u>Jonquiline</u>:
There's no sign of it.

Jessamine:
Oh! Oh! Jonquiline … it must have gone down the mouse-hole!

(The two sisters peer down the mousehole).

Jonquiline:
Oh, dear.

Jessamine:
I can't see it.

Jonquiliine:
It's dark in there.

Jessamine:
I can't get my hand inside.

Jonquiline:
It's lost.

Jessamine:
Completely lost. What shall we say to Beauty? Oh, my goodness, what will she say to us? Jonquiline ….

Jonquiline:
I cannot tell her. I cannot. She'll say I'm silly.

Jessamine:
We must make up a story.

Jonquiline:
Yes, but what?

Jessamine:
Don't cry, Jonquiline. If the ring is lost there's no use crying. And Beauty needn't know just how silly you … *(correcting herself)* … we …. have been this time.

<u>Jonquiline</u>:
What will you tell her?

<u>Jessamine</u>:
Now listen, Jonquiline … I shall say that a big bird flew through the window and carried the ring off the dressing-table, and away out into the night. A very big bird stole it.

<u>Jonquiline</u>:
But that isn't true.

<u>Jessamine</u>:
Well … it's not exactly a lie.

<u>Jonquiline</u>:
It sounds rather like a lie.

<u>Jessamine</u>:
Do you want to tell Beauty that you dropped it down a mouse-hole?

<u>Jonquiline</u>:
No, oh, no!

<u>Jessamine</u>:
Well, you see, a mouse has really stolen it. If I say it was a bird, instead of a mouse … well, a bird is only a bigger mouse with wings.

<u>Jonquiline</u>:
It sounds better now that you have explained it.

<u>Jessamine</u>:
Jonquiline, it's just gone ten o'clock.

<u>Jonquiline</u>:
And here comes Papa, with Beauty.

<u>Jessamine</u>:
Now, do be brave, Jonquiline.

THE LITTLE MERMAID
by Hans Christian Anderson

(The little mermaid lives under the sea in the kingdom of the Merpeople. She has fallen in love with a handsome prince. She asks an old witch for help to return to the world above the water. The witch lives in a marshy place where huge snails crawl about and in the middle stands a house built of bones of people who have been shipwrecked. The witch is sitting caressing a toad).

Witch:
I know exactly what you are going to ask me. Your wish is foolish, yet it shall be fulfilled though it is sure to bring misfortune on you, my fairest princess. You have come just at the right time. Had you come after sunset I wouldn't have been able to help you for another year. You must swim to land and sit down on the shore and swallow a drink which I will prepare for you. Your tail will then fall and shrink into the things which men call legs. This transformation will be very painful for you will feel as though a sharp knife has passed through your body. All who look on you will say that you are the loveliest child they have ever seen. You will keep all your graceful movements and no dancer will move so lightly. But - every step you take will cause you unbearable pain: it will be as though you were walking on the sharp edges of swords and your blood will flow. Can you endure all this suffering?

Mermaid:
Yes, I can.

Witch:
Then I will grant your request.

Mermaid:
Thank you. Thank you so much!

Witch:
Remember, that you can never be a mermaid again once you have received human form. You may never return to your sisters and your father's palace and unless you shall win the prince's love to such a degree that he shall leave his father and mother for you, that you shall

be part of all his thoughts and you become man and wife, you will never obtain the immortality you seek. Should he marry another you will die on the following day for your heart will break with sorrow and you will be changed to foam on the sea.

Mermaid:
Still, I will do it! I love him. So, I will do all that you say.

LITTLE RED RIDING HOOD
Adapted by Kim Gilbert

(Red Riding Hood is off to visit her Grandmother in the woods when she comes across a sly and greedy wolf).

<u>Red Riding Hood</u>:
Oh, you scared me. I didn't see you there!

<u>Wolf</u>:
I didn't mean to scare you, my dear. I saw you looking around and thought you might be lost.

<u>Red Riding Hood</u>:
Oh no! I know my way around these woods very well for my grandmother lives in the middle of them and I've been coming here for years to visit her. But today, I have brought her a special surprise as she has not been feeling well. My mother said for me to come and cheer her up and bring her some cakes and flowers.

<u>Wolf:</u>
What a kind and clever girl you are. What is your name?

<u>Red Riding Hood</u>:
My name is Red Riding Hood - on account of the red cape and bonnet which I always wear.

<u>Wolf:</u>
And a very fine cape and bonnet it is too!

<u>Red Riding Hood</u>:
Yes – my mother made it for me. And now you'll excuse me, if you don't mind, as I have to get going. My grandmother will be waiting for me and I want to arrive before it gets dark.

<u>Wolf:</u>
Why don't you let me come with you? I could help you. I could carry your basket.

Red Riding Hood:
No thankyou – it's quite all right. I can manage perfectly well.

Wolf:
I could show you where I live. My house is not far from here and there is a beautiful shady tree in my garden where you could take a rest?

Red Riding Hood:
No – thankyou. My grandmother is expecting me and she too has a beautiful garden. Now I really must be off. My mother is always telling me not to talk with strangers and whilst you seem very kind, I must obey my mother's wishes. Goodbye.

(Red Riding Hood skips off. The Wolf runs on ahead of her).

Wolf:
What a smart little girl! I'll overtake her and jump out on her just when she least suspects it!

Red Riding Hood:
Well, he was really quite a friendly wolf, as wolves go, although I didn't like the look of his big, sharp teeth! I really must get going – as it's beginning to get dark. Poor grandmama will be so relieved to see me and I'm looking forward to being able to help her whilst she's feeling poorly. Oh, look, primroses. Perhaps I'll stop and pick a small bunch to take to Grandmama. She loves primroses.

Wolf:
(He jumps out at Red Riding Hood.)
Well, fancy bumping into you again so soon. How lovely to see you again!

Red Riding Hood:
Oh, you frightened me! I thought you'd gone home.

Wolf:
Well, I couldn't bear the thought of you travelling all alone. I thought to myself "That poor little girl - all by herself. What if some nasty creature decided to jump out at her and steal her delicious goodies

– those goodies that she has so lovingly prepared for her sweet old Grannie. And then – what if that same nasty creature decided to follow her and break into her Grannie's and steal some of her precious things". No – of course, I could not allow you to travel alone. *(He smiles menacingly).*

Red Riding Hood:
(putting down her basket). Now, Wolfie – you have gone too far. I told you I was fine. I told you I know my way. And I told you I'm not allowed to talk to strangers. What I didn't tell you was – that I'm very good at karate! And so – if you won't take No for an answer – Take that! And that! And that!

Wolf:
Ow! Ow! Ow! I thought you were a sweet little girl!
(The wolf howls in pain and limps off).

Red Riding Hood:
Thank goodness Mother taught me how to look after myself! And now – off to see my grandmother.

ALICE IN WONDERLAND
by Lewis Carroll

(Alice has fallen asleep and her dream takes her to wonderland. On her journey she meets the Cheshire cat who keeps disappearing and is very rude).

<u>Alice:</u>
Cheshire Puss, would you tell me, please, which way I ought to go from here?

<u>Cat:</u>
That depends a good deal on where you want to get to.

<u>Alice:</u>
I don't much care where –

<u>Cat:</u>
Then it doesn't matter which way you go.

<u>Alice:</u>
So long as I get somewhere.

<u>Cat:</u>
Oh, you're sure to do that if you only walk long enough.

<u>Alice:</u>
What sort of people live about here?

<u>Cat:</u>
In that direction lives a Hatter: and in that direction lives a March Hare. Visit either you like: they're both mad.

<u>Alice:</u>
But I don't want to go among mad people.

<u>Cat:</u>
Oh, you can't help that, we're all mad here. I'm mad. You're mad.

Alice:
How do you now I'm mad?

Cat:
You must be or you wouldn't have come here.

Alice:
And how do you know that you're mad?

Cat:
To begin with, a dog's not mad. You grant that?

Alice:
I suppose so.

Cat:
Well, then, you see, a dog growls when it's angry, and wags its tail when it's pleased. Now, I growl when I'm pleased, and wag my tail when I'm angry. Therefore, I'm mad.

Alice:
I call it purring, not growling.

Cat:
Call it what you like. Do you play croquet with the Queen today?

Alice:
I should like it very much but I haven't been invited yet.

Cat:
You'll see me there. By the bye, what became of the Duchesses baby? I'd nearly forgotten to ask.

Alice:
It turned into a pig.

Cat:
I thought it would.
(The Cheshire cat vanishes).

Alice:
I've seen hatters before, the March Hare will be much the most interesting. Perhaps, as this is May, it won't be raving mad – at least not so mad as it was in March.

(The Cheshire cat appears suddenly again).

Cat:
Did you say pig, or fig?

Alice:
I said pig and I wish you wouldn't keep appearing and vanishing so suddenly; you make one quite giddy.

Cat:
All right. *(The Cheshire Cat leaves, just leaving his grin).*

Alice:
Well! I've often seen a cat without a grin, but a grin without a cat! It's the most curious thing I ever saw in all my life!

ALICE IN WONDERLAND
by Lewis Carroll

(Alice takes some advice from a caterpillar. They stare at each other for a few moments. The caterpillar speaks in a languid, sleepy voice).

Caterpillar:
Who are you?

Alice:
(shyly). I hardly know, sir, just at present – at least I know who I was when I got up this morning, but I think I must have been changed several times since then.

Caterpillar:
What do you mean by that? Explain yourself.

Alice:
I can't explain myself, I'm afraid, sir, because I am not myself, you see.

Caterpillar:
I don't see.

Alice:
I'm afraid I can't put it more clearly. For I can't understand it myself to begin with; and being so many different sizes in a day is very confusing.

Caterpillar:
It isn't.

Alice:
Well, perhaps you haven't found it so yet, but when you have to turn into a chrysalis – you will someday, you know – and then after that into a butterfly, I should think you'll feel it a little queer, won't you?

Caterpillar:
Not a bit.

Alice:
Well, perhaps your feelings may be different, all I know is, it would feel very queer to *me*.

Caterpillar:
You? Who are *you*?

Alice:
I think you ought to tell me who you are, first.

Caterpillar:
Why?

(Alice can't think of a good reason and as she finds the caterpillar very unpleasant, she turns away).

Caterpillar:
Come back! I've something important to say.

Alice:
This sounds promising. *(Alice turns back to face the caterpillar).*

Caterpillar:
Keep your temper.

Alice:
Is that all?

Caterpillar:
No. So you think you're changed, do you?

Alice:
I'm afraid I am, sir. I can't remember things as I used – and I don't keep the same size for ten minutes together.

Caterpillar:
Can't remember *what* things?

Alice:
Well, I've tried to say "How doth the little busy bee" but it all came out different.

Caterpillar:
Repeat 'You are old, Father William"

Alice:
'You are old, Father William,' the young man said,
'And your hair has become very white;
And yet you incessantly stand on your head –
Do you think, at your age, it is right?'

There's more.

Caterpillar:
That is not said right.

Alice:
Not *quite* right, I'm afraid, some of the words have got altered.

Caterpillar:
It is wrong from beginning to end. *(Silence).* What size do you want to be?

Alice:
Oh, I'm not particular as to size, only one doesn't like changing so often, you know.

Caterpillar:
I *don't* know. Are you content now?

Alice:
Well, I should like to be a *little* larger, sir, if you wouldn't mind, three inches is such a wretched height to be.

Caterpillar:
It is a very good height indeed. I am three inches!

Alice:
But I am not used to it! *(To herself)*. I wish creatures wouldn't be so easily offended.

Caterpillar:
You'll get used to it in time. *(He gets down off the mushroom on which he is sitting)*. One side will make you grow taller, and the other side will make you grow shorter.

Alice:
One side of *what*? The other side of *what*?

Caterpillar:
Of the mushroom.

(Alice looks thoughtfully at the mushroom, trying to make out which were the two sides of it as it was perfectly round. She puts her arm around the mushroom and breaks off a bit).

Alice:
And now, which is which? *(She takes a bite of the mushroom).*

ALICE IN WONDERLAND
By Lewis Carroll

(Alice finds her neck has grown so much that she is now peering up into a pigeon's nest. The pigeon thinks she is a serpent coming to steal her eggs).

Alice:
My head's free at last. What can all that green stuff be? And where have my shoulders got to? And, oh, my poor hands, how is it I can't see you?

(Suddenly a large pigeon flies into Alice's face and beats her violently with its wings).

Pigeon:
Serpent!

Alice:
I'm not a serpent! Let me alone!

Pigeon:
Serpent, I say again! *(sobbing).* I've tried every way, and nothing seems to suit them!

Alice:
I haven't the least idea what you're talking about.

Pigeon:
I've tried the roots of trees and I've tried branches and I've tried hedges, but those serpents! There's no pleasing them! As if it wasn't trouble enough hatching the eggs but I must be on the look-out for serpents night and day! Why, I haven't had a wink of sleep these three weeks!

Alice:
I'm very sorry you've been annoyed.

Pigeon:
And just as I'd taken the highest tree in the wood and just as I was thinking I should be free of them at last, they must needs come wriggling down from the sky! Ugh, Serpent!

Alice:
But I'm *not* a serpent, I tell you! I'm a – I'm a

Pigeon:
Well, *What* are you? I can see you're trying to invent something.

Alice:
I'm a little girl.

Pigeon:
A likely story indeed! *(spoken with contempt).* I've seen a good many little girls in my time, but never one with such a neck as that! No, no! You're a serpent; and there's no use denying it. I suppose you'll be telling me next that you never tasted an egg!

Alice:
I have tasted eggs, certainly, but little girls eat eggs quite as much as serpents do, you know.

Pigeon:
I don't believe it, but if they do, why then they're a kind of serpent, that's all I can say. You're looking for eggs, I know *that* well enough; and what does it matter to me whether you're a little girl or a serpent?

Alice:
It matters a good deal to me, but I'm not looking for eggs as it happens; and if I was, I shouldn't want *yours*; I don't like them raw.

Pigeon:
Well, be off, then! *(The pigeon settles down again on his/her nest).*

(Alice crouches down among the trees as best she can for her neck keeps getting caught in the branches. She takes out the mushroom which enables her to shrink and nibbles a piece of it until she brings herself down to her usual height).

Alice:
How puzzling all these changes are! I'm never sure what I'm going to be, from one minute to another! However, I've got back to my right size; the next thing is, to get into that beautiful garden – how is that to be done, I wonder?

HOW THE LEOPARD GOT HIS SPOTS BY RUDYARD KIPLING (1902)
Adapted by Kim Gilbert

(This story is from the Just So stories by Rudyard Kipling. They are a collection of stories to illustrate how animals obtained their particular attributes. An Ethiopian hunter paints spots on a leopard to help it blend into the shadows of the forest. The Ethiopian follows the animals to the forest. He also has dark skin so that he can hide in the shadows).

Leopard:
What is this that is so exclusively dark, and yet so full of little pieces of light?

Ethiopian:
I don't know but it ought to be the aboriginal Flora. I can smell Giraffe, and I can hear Giraffe, but I can't see Giraffe.

Leopard:
That's curious, I suppose it is because we have just come in out of the sunshine. I can smell Zebra, and I can hear Zebra, but I can't see Zebra.

Ethiopian:
Wait a bit, it's a long time since we've hunted them. Perhaps we've forgotten what they were like.

Leopard:
Fiddle. I remember them perfectly on the High Veldt, especially their marrow-bones. Giraffe is about seventeen feet high, of an exclusively golden-yellow from head to heel; and Zebra is about four and a half feet high, of an exclusively grey-fawn colour from head to heel.

Ethiopian:
Umm. Then they ought to show up in this dark place like ripe bananas in a smoke-house.

Leopard:
But we've hunted all day and they didn't. We could smell them and hear them, but we never saw one of them. Let us wait till it gets dark. This daylight hunting is a perfect scandal.

(So, they waited and the leopard heard something breathing).

It smells like Zebra, but I cannot see it. Be quiet, O you person without any form. I am going to sit on your head till morning, because there is something about you that I don't understand.

Ethiopian:
I've caught a thing that I can't see. It smells like Giraffe, and it kicks like Giraffe, but it hasn't any form.

Leopard:
Don't you trust it. Sit on his head till the morning – same as me. They haven't any form – any of them. It ought to be Zebra but it is covered with black and purple stripes. Don't you know that if you were on the High Veldt I could see you ten miles off? You haven't any form.

Ethiopian & Leopard:
All we can see are stripy shadows and blotched shadows in the forest, but never a sign of Zebra or Giraffe. It's like they have just walked off and hidden themselves in the shadowy forest.

Ethiopian:
That's a trick worth learning. Take a lesson by it, Leopard. You show up in this dark place like a bar of soap in a coal-scuttle.

Leopard:
Would it surprise you very much to know that you show up in this dark place like a mustard-plaster on a sack of coals?

Ethiopian:
Well, calling names won't catch dinner. The long and the short of it is that we don't match our backgrounds. I'm going to take Baviaan's advice. He told me I ought to change; and as I've nothing to change except my skin I'm going to change that.

Leopard:
What to?

Ethiopian:
To a nice working blackish-brownish colour, with a little purple in it, and touches of slaty-blue. It will be the very thing for hiding in hollows and behind trees. There – I have changed the colour of my skin!

Leopard:
But what about me? Baviaan's advice was to go into spots. So, I will. I will go into spots as fast as I can. I went into this spot with you, and a lot of good it has done me.

Ethiopian:
Baviaan didn't mean spots in South Africa. He meant spots on your skin.

Leopard:
What's the use of that?

Ethiopian:
Think of Giraffe, or if you prefer stripes, think of Zebra. They find their spots and stripes give them per-fect satisfaction.

Ethiopian:
Well, make up your mind, because I'd hate to go hunting without you, but I must if you insist on looking like a sunflower against a tarred fence.

Leopard:
I'll take spots, then, but don't make them too vulgar or big. I wouldn't look like Giraffe – not for ever so.

Ethiopian:
I'll make them with the tips of my fingers. There's plenty of black left on my new skin. I'll press them over you and wherever my five fingers touch they'll leave five little black marks, all close together. You can see them on any Leopard's skin you like. Sometimes my fingers may slip and the marks will be a little blurred; but if you look closely you will see that there are always five spots – from my five fat black finger-tips. *(He paints the spots on Leopard).* Now you are a beauty! You can lie out on the bare ground and look like a heap of pebbles. You can lie out on the naked rocks and look like a piece of pudding-stone. You can lie out on a leafy branch and look like sunshine sifting through the leaves; and you can lie right across the centre of the path and look like nothing particular. Think of that and purr!

Leopard:
But if I'm all this, why don't you go spotty too?

Ethiopian:
Plain black is best for me. Now let's go and see if we can go and get ourselves some breakfast.

HOW JAN KLASSEN CURED THE SICK KING
Adapted from an old Duth fairytale

(Kobus and Nelis are night watchmen to the king).

<u>Nelis:</u>
Now the day is nearly done!

<u>Kobus:</u>
In the sky now sets the sun,

<u>Nelis:</u>
Just as it has always done! I am Nelis, first nightwatchman to His Majesty, the King!

<u>Kobus:</u>
And I am Kobus, second nightwatchman to His Majesty, the king.

<u>Nelis:</u>
Night after night, we tramp the roads of Holland, keeping a sharp look out for robbers.

<u>Kobus:</u>
And thieves.

<u>Nelis:</u>
And highwaymen.

<u>Kobus:</u>
And pirates.

<u>Nelis:</u>
And dragons.

(The two nightwatchmen look around with lanterns in their hands).

<u>Kobus:</u>
Not a robber anywhere.

Nelis:
Not even a dragon. People can sleep safe in bed at night now we are watching the roads!

Kobus:
And a good thing too. For our King must not be bothered or worried.

Nelis:
His Majesty, the King is sick! He doesn't want to eat.

Nelis:
No appetite at all.

Kobus:
And such a headache!

Nelis:
The doctors have given him pills and powders.

Kobus:
And poultices and plasters.

Nelis:
And medicine, pink, blue and yellow.

Kobus:
But nothing does him any good.

Nelis:
Just makes him feel worse.

Kobus:
And now he doesn't know what to take or what to do. So tonight, we have a very important job to do. We have to stop and cry the sad news at every marketplace.

Nelis:
His Majesty, the King is sick. One thousand silver guilders will be gladly given to anyone who can cure the King. Please apply to the Royal Palace.

Kobus:
And then we have to hang notices like this on every tree. (*He produces a poster*). Now where shall I hang this one? Here? No, too high. Here? No, too low. This is a good place. We'll hang it here on this branch.

(*As Kobus turns around, he notices that Nelis has fallen asleep, leaving him to do all the work. Nelis is snoring*).

Kobus:
Asleep. You're a nightwatchman and you are asleep – at night! Wake up! Had a nice nap, Nightwatchman?

Nelis:
Nap? Nonsense. I was thinking. That's what I was doing. Thinking! I always think best with my eyes shut.

Kobus:
Then don't you dare think another thought till we get to Amsterdam. Start marching. Left, right, left, right, left, right. Off we march to Amsterdam. Left, right, left, right, left, right …

SNOW WHITE & THE SEVEN DWARVES
adapted from the fairy tale by Kim Gilbert

(The wicked Queen is jealous of her beautiful step-daughter, Snow White. Snow White is a pure, kind girl whilst her step-mother is not to be trusted).

Queen:
This child with her skin as white as snow and lips as red as cherries and jet black hair. The one her father calls Snow White. Little Snow White! How can she be possibly be lovelier than me. I'll ask my magic mirror.

Mirror, mirror, on the wall,
Who is the fairest of them all?

(She throws her shoe at the mirror).

You used to tell me 'I was the fairest queen of all' and now all you can say is

'You Oh Queen are beautiful, it is true, but Snow White is now much prettier than you'

I'll call for my huntsman and demand that he kills her. And he must bring me proof!

Snow White! Snow White!

Snow White:
Yes, step-mother? Did you want me? I thought I heard you talking to someone.

Queen:
Of course, I wasn't talking to someone. Really – do you think mirrors can speak!

Snow-White:
I have often heard a strange voice coming from your bed chamber. I must have been imagining things.

Queen:
Talking mirrors! I never heard the like.

Snow White:
What did you want me for, step-mother?

Queen:
You are going on a trip to the forest. My faithful huntsman will accompany you. Be sure you to stay close to him. There are wild wolves at large who would eat you for their dinner. But the Huntsman will protect you – he is big and strong - so be sure to stay close to him.

Snow-White:
That's strange, step-mother. You don't usually allow me to leave the castle grounds. How wonderful to go on a trip. Is there anything you would like me to bring back for you? I'm sure there are some wonderful wild flowers there. Perhaps I could pick some for you. They would brighten up your room.

Queen:
Wild flowers! Yes – that would be delightful. What a kind, and thoughtful girl you are.

Snow-White:
It would be a pleasure. I'm so pleased that you are allowing me some freedom. Perhaps we can become friends and spend some time together. I'd like that. I've been so lonely here since my mother died.

Queen:
Yes – well, we can talk about that if you - when you return, my dear. Be sure to stay close to the Huntsman.

THE BLUE BIRD
by Maurice Maeterlink

(The Bluebird is a story of a brother and sister who help a little girl whose illness can only be cured by the magical Blue Bird of Happiness. To find the bird, Mytyl and Tyltyl quest through the Land of Memory to the Palace of Night. In this scene, Tyltyl meets a young child who has not yet been born).

Tyltyl:
How do you do? *(touching the child's blue dress).* What's that?

Child:
(touching Tyltyl's hat). And what's that?

Tyltyl:
That. That's my hat. Have you no hat?

Child:
No. What is it for?

Tyltyl:
It's to say how-do-you-do with. And then for when it's cold.

Child:
What does that mean, when it's cold?

Tyltyl:
When you shiver like this: brrr! When you blow into your hands and go like this with your arms. *(He beats his arm across his chest).*

Child:
Is it cold on Earth?

Tyltyl:
Yes, sometimes, in the winter, when there is no fire.

Child:
Why is there no fire?

Tyltyl:
Because it is expensive and it costs money to buy wood.

Child:
What is money?

Tyltyl:
It's what you pay with.

Child:
Oh!

Tyltyl:
Some people have money and others have none.

Child:
Why?

Tyltyl:
Because they are not rich. Are you rich? How old are you?

Child:
I am going to be born soon. I shall be born in twelve years. Is it nice to be born?

Tyltyl:
Oh yes! It's great fun!

Child:
How did you manage?

Tyltyl:
I can't remember. It's so long ago!

Child:
They say it's lovely, the Earth and the Live People!

Tyltyl:
Yes, it's not bad. There are birds and cakes and toys. Some have them all; but those who have none can look at the others.

Child:
They tell us that the mothers stand waiting at the door. They are good, aren't they?

Tyltyl:
Oh yes! They are better than anything in the world. And the grannies too, but they die too soon.

Child:
They die? What is that?

Tyltyl:
They go away one evening and do not come back.

Child:
Why?

Tyltyl:
How can one tell? Perhaps because they feel sad.

Child:
Has yours gone?

Tyltyl:
My grandmamma?

Child:
Your mamma or your grandmamma, I don't know.

Tyltyl:
Oh, but it's not the same thing! The grannies go first, that's sad enough. Mine was very kind to me.

Child:
What is the matter with your eyes? Are they making pearls?

<u>Tyltyl:</u>
No, it's not pearls.

<u>Child:</u>
What is it, then?

<u>Tyltyl:</u>
It's nothing, it's all that blue which dazzles me a little.

<u>Child:</u>
What is that called? There, that, falling down.

<u>Tyltyl:</u>
Nothing. It's a little water.

<u>Child:</u>
Does it come from the eyes?

<u>Tyltyl:</u>
Yes, sometimes, when one cries.

<u>Child:</u>
What does that mean, crying?

<u>Tyltyl:</u>
I have not been crying, it is the fault of that blue. But, if I had cried, it would be the same thing.

<u>Child:</u>
Does one often cry?

<u>Tyltyl:</u>
Not little boys, but little girls do. Don't you cry here?

<u>Child:</u>
No, I don't know how.

Tyltyl:
Well, you will learn. What are you playing with, those great blue wings?

Child:
These? That's for the invention which I shall make on Earth.

Tyltyl:
What invention? Have you invented something?

Child:
Why, yes, haven't you heard? When I am on Earth, I shall have to invent the thing that gives happiness.

Tyltyl:
Is it good to eat? Does it make a noise?

Child:
No, you hear nothing.

Tyltyl:
That's a pity.

Child:
I work at it every day. It is almost finished. Would you like to see it?

Tyltyl:
Very much. Where is it?

Child:
There, you can see it from here, between those two columns. Thirty three remedies for prolonging life. There, in those blue phials are thirty three children. All these children must take something with them to Earth: the children are not allowed to go from here empty handed.

Tyltyl:
Who says so?

<u>Child:</u>
Time, who stands at the door. You will see when he opens it.

THE TOWN MOUSE & THE COUNTRY MOUSE
Adapted from Aesops Fables by Kim Gilbert

(This scene is adapted from one of Aesop's many fables. A Town Mouse and a Country Mouse invite each other to dinner).

Country Mouse:
Dear cousin from the town. Welcome to my humble abode. Please come in and share with me all I have to offer. I have beans and bacon, cheese and bread. Please dine with me and eat to your hearts content.

(The two mice sit and share some supper together).

Country Mouse:
Can I tempt you with some fine country ale, cousin?

Town Mouse:
Ale? Do you not serve wine in your house, cousin?

Country Mouse:
The ale is the finest the country offers. Try it before you judge, dear cousin.

Town Mouse:
Thank you, dear friend. But I cannot understand Cousin, how you can put up with such poor food as this - but I suppose one cannot expect anything better in the country. Come with me next time to the town and I will show you how to live. When you have been in town for a week you will wonder how you could ever have stood a country life.

Country Mouse:
Dear cousin, indeed, next time, I will pay you a visit at your elegant abode in the town. I very much look forward to it.

(Next scene. The following week the Country Mouse visits his cousin in town).

Town Mouse:
Dear cousin, from the country. You will need some refreshment after your long journey. Come and see my grand dining room and you will see the fine feast I have laid on for you.

Country Mouse:
Why thank you, dear cousin. I would be delighted. I am hungry from my journey and look forward to a hearty supper with you.

Town Mouse:
We have fine wines and meats. Cake and jellies galore! Take your pick. Feast your eyes and your stomach on the finest fare this town has to offer.

Country Mouse:
Don't mind if I do. I must say, your spread is very tempting with so much to choose from. I don't know which to choose first. Now I can see *why* you have a much larger waistline than mine.

Town Mouse:
A fat stomach is a healthy stomach. Surely a sign of wealth and good fortune.

Country Mouse:
After this banquet, I fear I may need a sleep. I'm not sure I will have enough energy to be able to climb the stairs.

(Suddenly a loud sound of dogs barking is heard. Two large bull mastiffs enter fiercely).

Country Mouse:
What's that?

Town Mouse:
Oh, it is only the dogs of the house. You'll soon get used to them.

Country Mouse:
Only! I do not like that 'music' at my dinner table. I fear I would never get used to them.

<u>Town Mouse</u>:
Do not worry, dear cousin. These are just things you have to learn to cope with when you are living in the town.

<u>Country Mouse:</u>
I don't think I have the strength and energy to run away. I'm sorry dear cousin from the town, but better beans and bacon in peace than cake and wine eaten in fear.

THE HARE AND THE TORTOISE
Adapted by Kim Gilbert from the fable by Aesop

(The boastful Hare thinks he is the best and fastest runner of all the animals. Little does he know that plodding can also win the race).

Hare:
I have never yet been beaten in my whole life. I am the fastest of all the animals when I put forth my full speed. I challenge any one here to race with me.

Tortoise:
I accept your challenge.

Hare:
That is a good joke, tortoise. I could dance round you all the way – no matter the place, time or day.

Tortoise:
Keep your boasting till you've beaten. There are many ways to catch a monkey, as the saying goes. What's say we race?

Hare:
That's an easy challenge. I'll beat you in no time.

Tortoise:
We'll soon see you pompous Hare. I may be slow but I will get there in the end.

(Hare starts to sprint around a track whilst tortoise slowly plods along, one foot in front of the other).

Hare:
Tortoise doesn't know what he's talking about. How could he possibly think of beating me? What a stupid challenge! I think I'll take a nap. I've got heaps of time on my hands.
I think I'll lie down behind this lovely shady bush.

(Hare settles himself down behind a bush and soon falls asleep).

Tortoise:
No sign of hare. Arrogant fellow! Still, someone needs to show him. I know I can get around this track even though it might take me a little longer. I'll just take my time. Anyway, taking my time means I get to appreciate the finer things in life. What lovely flowers over there! And just look at those butterflies! Oh, and there's Mr Sparrow. Hello Mr Sparrow. Lovely day!

(Tortoise continues to slowly plod around the track).

Now, what have we here? Mr Hare, fast asleep! Well, Well, Well! Now I'll show him. Goodbye Mr Hare. See you at the finishing line. Enjoy your nap! Now - just one more lap.

Hare:
What a glorious dream I've been having. I needed that nap. Now to get on with the race. Tortoise will still be behind. He is so S-L-O -W! I can beat him easily.

(Hare starts to sprint and suddenly sees Tortoise almost at the finishing line).

Hey, tortoise – wait up! How can this have happened? I'll have to sprint faster. Just a bit more effort – run faster – *(panting)*.

Tortoise:
I don't think you can catch me up, Hare. I'm almost there. Just a few more steps.

Hare:
This can't be happening. Tortoise is going to beat me!

Tortoise:
Done it! And without too much effort too. And the crowd are cheering me! Thanks everyone. Thanks for your support!

Hare:
I can't believe it. That's not fair. You cheated!

Tortoise:
How did I cheat? It's not my fault you decided to have a sleep?

Hare:
Grrr!

Tortoise:
Well – you called me a plodding old tortoise. But it just goes to show – plodding can win the race!

THE LION, THE WITCH & THE WARDROBE
BY C.S. LEWIS

(The four children are in the land of Narnia and have met Mr Beaver. He has decided to take them home to see his wife at their dam and where they will be able to talk in private).

Mr Beaver:
Let's go home to Mrs Beaver. Follow me. Here we are. The sluice gate's very old and rickety. You can't get the Timber since SHE came to power. Mrs Beaver! Mrs Beaver! I've found them! The children. They're here!

(Mr Beaver & the children enter Beaver's house).

Mrs Beaver:
So - you've come at last. To think that ever I should see the day. The potatoes are on the boil and the kettle soon will be. And I daresay, Mr Beaver, as you'll get us some fish?

Mr Beaver:
Business afore pleasure, Mrs Beaver. Business afore pleasure.

Mrs Beaver:
Well, do sit down, my dears.

Mr Beaver:
What happened to Mr Tumnus? That's a very bad business indeed. There's no doubt that he was taken off by Maugrim the Wolf. I heard that from a bird who saw it being done. He's been taken Northwards.

Mrs Beaver:
And we all know what that means! Of course, you don't. I'm afraid it means Maugrim was taking Tumnus to her house.

Mr Beaver:
There's not many taken in that ever comes out again, not from that house. All full of statues it is. In the courtyard, up the stairs, and all over the big hall. People as she's turned to stone. With her magic wand.

Mrs Beaver:
Her magic wand … Save Mr Tumnus? I don't doubt you'd save him if you could, dearie, but you've no chance of getting into that house against her will and ever coming out again.

Mr Beaver:
Ah yes. But now that Aslan is on the move ….

Mr Beaver:
Aslan is the King. The Lord of the whole wood, as far as I know.

Mrs Beaver:
But he's not often here you see.

Mr Beaver:
Never before in my time, nor my father's either.

Mrs Beaver:
But the word is out that he's back. He's back in Narnia to settle the White Witch! If the White Witch can stand on her own two feet and look him in the face, it'll be a miracle. There's a well-known saying:-

Mr Beaver:
Wrong will be right, when Aslan comes in sight.

Mrs Beaver:
At the sound of his roar, sorrows will be no more.
When he bares his teeth, winter meets it's death.

Mr Beaver:
When he shakes his mane, we shall ... we shall have Spring again!

That's why I brought you all here. Now that Tumnus is her prisoner. I've been chosen to lead the four of you to Aslan.

Mrs Beaver:
Oh, no, dear! He isn't a man!

Mr Beaver:
Certainly not! He is the King of the wood.

Mrs Beaver:
Haven't you heard of the King of the Beasts? Aslan is a lion. A great lion! You may feel rather nervous about meeting a lion. But don't worry, dearie, I'll be with you.

Mr Beaver:
Word has been sent that you are to meet him tomorrow, if you can, at the Stone Table. There is a prophecy. Over at Cair Paravel, a castle, the Capital of Narnia, there are 4 thrones.

Mrs Beaver:
Yes – 4 thrones! And the prophecy says …

'When two Sons of Adam, two Daughters of Eve,
Sit on the four thrones, for all to believe,
The White Witch will die, her wicked reign will cease.'

Mr & Mrs Beaver:
Forever.

(silence).

Mrs Beaver:
Where's Edmund? Edmund? Edmund … Edmund…

Mr Beaver:
Will you calm down everyone? There's no point panicking. There's no point panicking because if we think hard we already know where he's gone. He's gone to her. To the White Witch. He has betrayed us to her. You mark my words – he has met the White Witch - joined her side.

Mrs Beaver:
What she wants is to get all four of you inside her house. Then she'll turn you into statues. Like Tumnus. She'll keep your brother alive as long as he's the only one she's got. She'll use him as a decoy, as bait to catch the rest of you with.

Mr Beaver:
Only Aslan can help us. So - we must go on and meet him.

Mrs Beaver:
We must all get away from here. There's not a moment to lose

Mr Beaver:
And now we must all be moving off, to the Stone Table.

Mrs Beaver:
Come on, my dearies. It's a long way to go, and she won't be far behind. That's strange … I thought I heard water trickling off the roof. Whoever heard of water running in Narnia? Come, let's go!

MAKE BELIEVE
BY A. A. MILNE

(Despite the King trying to find a prince to marry his daughter, the princess has decided to marry a woodcutter).

The Princess:
Good morning, Woodcutter.

Woodcutter:
Good morning. *(He continues with his work).*

Princess:
Don't you ever say anything except Good Morning?

Woodcutter:
Sometimes I say good-bye.

Princess:
You *are* a cross woodcutter today You are still cutting wood? Don't you ever do anything else?

Woodcutter:
Well, you are still a Princess; and don't you ever do anything else?

Princess:
Now that's not fair, Woodcutter. You can't say I was a Princess yesterday, when I came and helped you stack your wood. Or the day before, when I tied up your hand where you had cut it. Or the day before that, when we had our meal together on the grass. Was I a Princess then?

Woodcutter:
Perhaps I'm just as bad as you. Only yesterday I was thinking to myself how unselfish I was to interrupt my work in order to talk to a mere Princess.

Princess:
The trouble is that you *don't* interrupt your work.

Woodcutter:
Madam, I am at your service.

Princess:
I wish I thought you were.

Woodcutter:
Surely you have enough people at your service already. Princes and Chancellors and Chamberlains and Waiting Maids.

Princess:
Yes, that's just it. That's why I want your help. Particularly in the matter of Princes.

Woodcutter:
Why, has a suitor come for the hand of her Royal Highness?

Princess:
Three suitors. And I hate them all.

Woodcutter:
And which are you going to marry?

Princess:
I don't know. Father hasn't made up his mind yet.

Woodcutter:
And this is a matter which father – which His Majesty decides for himself?

Princess:
Of course. You should read the history books, Woodcutter. The suitors to the hand of a Princess are always set some trial of strength or test of quality by the King and the winner marries his daughter.

Woodcutter:
Well, I don't live in a Palace, and I think my own thoughts about these things. I'd better get back to my work.

(He continues chopping).

Princess:
Woodcutter!

Woodcutter:
Oh, are you there? I thought you were married by this time.

Princess:
I don't want to be married. *(Quickly).* I mean, not to any of those three. That's why I wanted *you* to help me.

Woodcutter:
Can a simple woodcutter help a Princess?

Princess:
Well, perhaps a simple one couldn't, but a clever one might.

Woodcutter:
What would his reward be?

Princess:
His reward would be that the Princess, not being married to any of her three suitors, would still be able to help him chop his wood in the mornings … I *am* helping you, aren't I?

Woodcutter:
Decidedly! It is kind of a great lady like yourself to help so humble a fellow as I.

Princess:
I'm not very great.

Woodcutter:
There is enough of you to make a hundred men unhappy.

Princess:
And one man very happy.

Woodcutter:
And one man very, very happy.

Princess:
Woodcutter, if *you* were a Prince, would you be my suitor? Would you kill the others? With that axe? That's where you'll have the advantage of them when it comes to axes.

Woodcutter:
I would not kill them, in order to help His Majesty make up his mind about his son-in-law. But if the Princess had made up her mind – and wanted me – then I would marry her, however many suitors she had.

Princess:
Well, she's only got three at present.

Woodcutter:
What is that to me?

Princess:
Oh, I just thought you might want to be doing something to your axe.

Woodcutter:
My axe?

Princess:
Yes. You see, she h*as* made up her mind.

Woodcutter:
But – you mean – But I'm only a woodcutter.

Princesses:
That's where you'll have the advantage of them when it comes to axes.

Woodcutter:
Princess! My Princess!

Princess:
Woodcutter! My Woodcutter! My, oh so very slow and uncomprehending, but entirely adorable woodcutter!

Woodcutter:
But what will his Majesty say?

Princess:
All sorts of things. Do you really love me, Woodcutter, or have I proposed to you under a misapprehension? If I had been a simple peasant, I suppose you would have said it a long time ago?

Woodcutter:
I adore you!

Princess:
I thought you did. But I wanted to hear you say it. If I had been a simple peasant, I suppose you would have said it a long time ago? Well, now we must think of a plan for making Mother like you.

Author Index

The Little Mermaid by H.C. Anderson (1837)

The Three Little Pigs adapted by K. Gilbert

Snow White & the Seven Dwarves by K.Gilbert

by Hans Christian Anderson (1837)

Peter Pan by J.M. Barrie (1911)

The Wizard of Oz by L. Frank Baum (1900)

Alice in Wonderland by Lewis Carroll (1865)

Puss in Boots by Perrault (1697)

Toad of Toad Hall by Kenneth Grahame (1929)

The House at Pooh Corner by A.A.Milne

The Lion, the Witch & the Wardrobe by C.S.Lewis (1950)

Make Believe by A.A. Milne (1925)

Tom Sawyer by Mark Twain (1876)

Pinocchio by Carlo Collodi (1883)

Puss in Boots by Charles Perrault (1697)

How the Leopard got his spots by Rudyard Kipling (1902) adapted by K. Gilbert

Aesops Fables adapted by K. Gilbert

The Poppenkast – Dutch fairy tale

The Blue Bird by M. Maeterlink (1908)

Winnie the Pooh by A. A. Milne (1926)

Beauty & the Beast by Barbot de Villeneuve

About the Author

Kim Gilbert trained as a professional actress at the Guildford School of Acting, studied for an LGSM with the Guildhall School of Music and Drama and took an English degree at the Open University. She has been acting, teaching and directing plays and musical productions for more than 35 years. She has experience in a wide range of theatre, TV and voiceover work. She has a First-class Honours degree in English and has taught English and Drama in many top schools in the country. Kim examined for Lamda for a number of years and has also acted as an adjudicator. She has been running Dramatic Arts Studio for 13yrs, a private drama studio which specialises in developing excellence in all forms of performance and communication.

Other Books by the same author:

Shakespeare Scenes
Monologues for young adult female actors
Monologues for young female actors
Duologues for female actors
Monologues for young male actors

Chekhov Scenes
Monologues & Duologues for women
Monologues for Male Actors

Scenes from Oscar Wilde
Monologues & Duologues for female actors
Monologues for Male actors
Duologues from Oscar Wilde

Scenes from George Bernard Shaw
Monologues & duologues for male & female actors

Classic Scenes
Classic Monologues for female actors
Classic Duologues for female actors
Classical Scenes: Monologues for Male Actors
Classic Acting Monologues for Girls (8-14yrs)
Classic Acting Monologues for Boys (8-14yrs)
Classic Duologues for Boys & Girls (8-14yrs)
Acting Monologues for girls (aged 5-10yrs)

Contemporary Duologues for girls
Shakespeare's plots adapted for a modern world

Improve Your Voice
How to speak English with confidence

All available from Amazon Bookstore

Thank you for reading! If you enjoyed this book or found it useful, I would be grateful if you'd post a short review on Amazon. Your support really does make a difference and I read all the reviews personally so I can get your feedback and make this book even better. Thanks again for your support

Printed in Great Britain
by Amazon